S H A

SHAW

by

J. S. COLLIS

KENNIKAT PRESS
Port Washington, N. Y./London

SHAW

First published in 1925
Reissued in 1972 by Kennikat Press
Library of Congress Catalog Card No: 70-160748
ISBN 0-8046-1561-6

Manufactured by Taylor Publishing Company   Dallas, Texas

CONTENTS

CHAP.		PAGE
	NOTE	7
	PREFACE	9
I	A VOICE FOR IRELAND	11
II	THE NEW MISTAKE ABOUT BERNARD SHAW: HIS NEW AUDIENCE: HIS NEW DANGER	17
III	'GONE OUT AND GONE WRONG'	29
IV	DIVINATION: GOD: THE DIVINITY THAT SHAPES OUR ENDS: SHAW'S MESSAGE TO NORMAL MAN	41
V	THE BUILDER: THE IMMORALIST: THE TORY	50
VI	SHAVIAN EDUCATION	60
VII	NO 'REAL' BERNARD SHAW: THE SWORD THAT SLEW THE SLAYER: PARNASSUS: ON THE PLATFORM	67
VIII	THE SOUL OF DRAMA: THE DESTINY OF CHARACTERISATION: TECHNIQUE: UNDERSHAFT'S PROFESSION: THE MEANING OF HEARTBREAK HOUSE	99
IX	COMMON-SENSE ABOUT SHAW'S WORKMANSHIP: THE NARRATOR WE HAVE LOST	145
X	COMMON-SENSE ABOUT SHAW'S 'ORIGINALITY'	163
XI	COMMON-SENSE ABOUT SHAW'S 'IMMORTALITY'	170
XII	CONCLUSION	178

NOTE

I am indebted to Mr. Shaw for kindly allowing me to use as footnotes a few of the comments which he made on the original MS.

J. S. C.

PREFACE

SOME books are written for the pleasure of the reader and the profit of the writer, some for the profit of the reader and the pleasure of the writer, and some simply insist upon being written in spite of reader and writer. The latter sort, as Samuel Butler complained, are often a great nuisance to the writer as well as to everybody else, but nevertheless they must be written. This is such a book. It is therefore not possible for me to make the usual apology for the appearance of a new book on an old subject.

SHAW

CHAPTER ONE

A Voice for Ireland

★

IT happens that I am an Irishman, and I consider it to be time that Ireland had something to say about the most remarkable man who has ever fled from her shores. When Mr. Sean O'Casey, the young Irish playwright, said recently that he did not think that Shaw was properly appreciated in England but that it must be acknowledged that in Ireland he was not appreciated at all, he spoke no less than the truth. It would be wrong to say that in Ireland no one has ever heard of Shaw; but with obvious exceptions it can be said with strict accuracy that the vast majority if they mention his name at all mention it only with a sneer. He is despised as a fool by the foolish, considered a crank by the more intelligent, and disliked by the jealous. In January 1923, when Ireland celebrated her new-born freedom by introducing a Flogging Bill, Bernard Shaw wrote a letter to the *Irish Times* complaining against such barbarity. I was in Ireland at the time and I heard a number of the members of the Dail mention the letter. 'Oh, it's only Shaw!' they said. 'He is anti-everything: anti-flogging, anti-vaccination, anti-vivisection. His facts are all wrong. Flogging *works*.'

In other quarters they said cheerfully, 'He is just a crank'. With a few obvious exceptions Ireland is still at the 'tongue-in-his-cheek' stage as regards Bernard Shaw.

But I think this attitude towards him can be traced at bottom to two reasons. First, because he freely criticises Ireland; second, because he is a successful man — two unforgivable sins to an Irishman. The Irish cannot bear criticism; for like all races who have been oppressed they are still without mental bravery. They are afraid to see themselves exposed to what they imagine to be adverse criticism. That is why they feel indignant at the Third Act of *John Bull's Other Island*: that is why *The Playboy of the Western World* was frantically boycotted by people who were so enraged that they did not notice that the hero is admired not because he is a murderer but because he is a fine fellow who can tell 'a gallous story' rather than do 'a dirty deed'. Moreover, in strong contrast to the English, they are the most insular nation in the world. The English do not much care for their own country. They are more interested in lands beyond the seas, in kingdoms which they cannot conquer, and in dominions which they cannot hold. Their schoolmasters produce maps with places daubed in blood-colour that 'belong to England', their clergymen collect subscriptions from Boys Clubs in the East End of London for the clothing of Hindu children, and their government holds Exhibitions in which the wealth of these countries is shown, while everyone knows that England remains as neglected as ever with agricultural labourers getting twenty-five shillings a week and hospitals subsisting on the chances of charity.

From this lack of insularity the Irish swing to the opposite extreme. They are sufficient unto themselves. Not only have they no desire to take up a White Man's Burden (which in prose means 'look after anyone's business rather than your own') but they have no desire to share anything with anyone else. They do not want to share even their literature with any other nation. In spite of the fact that English has always been such a mighty instrument in their hands, in spite of the fact that the Nobel Prize has been awarded to their national poet, in spite of the fact that Ireland has supplied English Literature with nearly all its greatest playwrights with the possible exception of Shakespeare (who was probably an Irishman), they are now advocating the return to Gaelic. This monstrous insult to a country's intellectual men and to the cosmopolitan message of art could only be countenanced by a people who are cowards at heart. They fear the insecurity of sharing anything. They want to commandeer everything for themselves. 'They would,' as an accomplished Irishman once said to me, 'commandeer God if they could.' It is therefore scarcely surprising that an Irishman like Bernard Shaw to whom boundaries are but bandages on the struggling body of humanity, and whose contempt for and criticism of Ireland's selfishness is freely expressed, finds himself without honour in his own country.

The second reason for Shaw's failure in Ireland is due to his success elsewhere. Those who are acquainted with his success are jealous of him. The Irish are the most jealous nation alive – again in strong contrast to the success-worshipping Englishman. The English are always ready to help a promising young man, but the Irish will deliberately baulk the career of a young man for no better reason than because he is promising. Every accomplished Irishman considers that he himself is the pick of his circle and will bear no brother near the throne. If anyone doubts this let him watch the proceedings from the inside of any Irish Society in Ireland or England, let him ask himself why it is that since the days of Phelim O'Neil until to-day Irishmen have never been able to co-operate on any single occasion, let him observe the fate which pursues the Irish Players and leads to their destruction. Jealousy, perhaps even more than the force of Religion and the follies of England, has moulded the course of Irish History. Bernard Shaw's success outside Ireland is sufficient to account for his neglect inside.

I hasten to add that though I have thus laid stress upon two unpleasing Irish characteristics because to a certain extent they explain Ireland's indifference to Mr. Shaw, it would be easy to mention qualities which may outweigh such faults. But the future of Ireland largely depends upon how much she is prepared to listen to criticism and how far she is capable of preserving peace between able men.

To return then to Bernard Shaw, with the exception of certain articles all criticism of him has so far come from English or foreign pens. My voice may remedy this. Though now a Londoner I have lived in the same atmosphere and bathed on the same beach during my boyhood as he did during his. Nevertheless, I am happy to say that I have no special 'theory' to offer about him. My qualification for writing this book is simply that when I was a schoolboy I saw *John Bull's Other Island* performed at the Abbey Theatre before I had ever heard of Shaw. Never will I forget that evening! I was sixteen — that frightful age, that no-man's-land, between childhood and manhood when you don't know where you are or what you are, and look up for help and guidance to fools and bullies and liars and cheats. The play was acted by the best set of Irish Players that have ever worked together at the Abbey Theatre — perfect beyond perfection. I heard the voice of Keegan; I listened to the heavenly music — and I knew that at last I was feeling the real thing. I forgot that I was sixteen: I knew only that I was listening to words that I fain would have uttered, to thoughts which were surely mine. In that hour I saw straight into the soul of Bernard Shaw and the opinion of him which I then formed has ever since been increasingly justified.

CHAPTER TWO

The New Mistake about Bernard Shaw: His New Audience: His New Danger

*

I

WE can find plenty of reasons to support any view in which we wish to believe. This well-known fact is illustrated by the present attitude of the English public towards Bernard Shaw. He is receiving much praise. This praise is chiefly due, however, to the belief that he has changed, not that we have changed. That he has come round to us, not that we have come round to him. It is generally believed that he started his career in London as the reddest of red revolutionaries, knocking everything down, insulting everybody, smashing, gibing, blaspheming, kicking at everything until he woke up one morning to find himself infamous throughout Europe; that for long years he held the position of cynic, mocker, iconoclast, paradox-monger, and atheist, whom it would be ridiculous to take seriously; but that lately, under the influence of declining years, he has changed his tone, taken to religion, and become a gentle satirist, a less revolutionary thinker, a mystic, an altogether milder man.

Many things seem to support this belief. It is supported by the attitude of the Church of England towards him. We hear eminent clergymen at intervals declare that he is our greatest spiritual teacher, we discover deputations sent to him from the staff of St. Martin's-in-the-Fields asking about knotty points in Theology, and we see (as I write these lines) the pit and stalls of the New Theatre being filled by all kinds of clergymen come to see *Saint Joan*. And if the behaviour of the Church towards him seems to show that he has become milder in his religious views, his behaviour towards the Labour Party would seem to show that he has become less revolutionary in his politics. For though he knows perfectly well that the Labour Party is not a revolutionary party, and shows us whenever it gets a chance that it does not even dream of doing anything that would shock a landowner in the Dark Ages were he alive, he nevertheless shows no impatience with it like Mr. H. G. Wells, but backs it up with unfailing energy on every possible occasion. Finally, as if to prove that he has become thoroughly respectable, he has changed his brown suit for a black one and his red beard for a white one. Therefore it is felt by thousands of respectable people who would have nothing to do with the old Bernard Shaw that a man with such a patriarchal aspect and proper views can be safely admired in private and applauded in public.

But they are wrong. They were hideously wrong about the past Bernard Shaw and are now making a new mistake about the present one. They imagined that when he was young he was hard, cynical and inhuman, though every page of his four published novels revealed a dangerously sensitive and humane mind: they believed that when he was in his prime he was insincere and irreligious though every play preached the same religion as *Saint Joan* with the same sincerity as in *Back to Methuselah*. So it is not surprising that they now think that he has become mellowed with age. Nothing could be farther from the truth. He has become not less but more revolutionary. He is a perfect example of the truth of his own saying that 'the most distinguished persons become more revolutionary as they grow older, though they are commonly supposed to become more conservative owing to their loss of faith in conventional methods of reform'. It is true that he backs up the Labour Party. But that is only because he considers that it is the best party that could exist under the circumstances, and rather than sit down and do nothing to help, he gives it all the encouragement he can. But politically speaking his thoughts are not their thoughts. He has no genuine belief that there can be a gradual transition from Capitalism to Socialism as contemplated by Sidney Webb. He used to believe that such a transition was possible in his early days when he wrote his contributions to the Fabian Essays, but since that time he has swung much more to the Left and now out-Lenins the Leninites in his advocation of Communism. In his recent *Dictatorship of the Proletariat* he dismisses the possibility of slow transition under present institutions by saying that 'Messrs. Henderson and Clynes can no more make our political machine produce socialism than they can make a sewing machine produce fried eggs'. He goes farther than Saint Paul, the first socialist, who said 'If a man does not work, neither shall he eat,' and says, 'If a man does not work, neither shall he live' — thus ruthlessly attacking Trade Unions that encourage ca' canny and launch strikes. He insists that if a man does not willingly work for two hours a day to justify his existence in the world then he must be forced to do so. This banishment of Liberty goes under the modern name of Bolshevism. At a recent meeting at which Mr. Shaw was speaking upon this subject some one asked him 'Are you a Bolshevik? If not, why not?' He replied simply 'I am a Bolshevik'. Again it is true that he is received well by the Church of England. But that is not because he has in any way changed his view of religion: it is because the Church having lost all faith in itself and all influence over the people is only too ready to turn to any man with a spiritual message. The fact that they are ready to turn to the author of *Androcles and the Lion* only proves again that they hate the dogmas in which they are supposed to believe. Finally, it is true that Shaw's personal appearance has considerably changed. But let no man be mistaken in that change! His beard was once red-hot with anger: it is now white-hot with rage.

II

The fact remains, however, that his audience has greatly changed in the last few years both in age and in appreciation. The kind and humane people who thought him cruel and inhuman; the religious people who thought him irreligious; the brave who thought him cowardly; the great who thought him small; the learned who thought him ignorant; the saintly who thought him unworthy of regard; the respectable who thought him a low fellow, have now practically all vanished after having demonstrated yet again the fact that a great, a noble, and a cultured innovator is always attacked at first more violently and bitterly by the great, the noble, and the cultured than by any other people. There are still of course some gallant die-hards who stick to their old view of him just as there are still some of the famous 'tongue-in-his-cheek' people who occasionally surprise us by their once familiar chirp. There are still some ladies who 'don't know when he is serious and when he is not', just as there are still some clean-living, robust-thinking, athletic 'good fellows' who think him 'cynical'. I have met all these people many times over, and have again and again been routed and cowed before that strange power which is given alone to the invincibly stupid.

There is a certain time in one's life (I think it is just before the dawn of manhood) when one subconsciously worries about apparent inconsistencies. One wonders vaguely why it is that everyone praises Jesus but runs down the Jews; why it is that the parson in Church says at one moment that God is a jealous God and visits the sins of fathers upon their children and then later says that God is a God of love and in no way like the other God he mentioned earlier in the service; why people consider it proper to be undressed on the sea-shore but improper to be undressed on the road to the sea-shore; why the Government pays the Soldier to shield us, the Law to judge us, and the Schools to teach us but does not pay the Hospitals to heal us, and so on. I remember wondering at this time why it was that Shaw, so obviously sentimental and humane, should be considered hard and cynical by my betters. For some time I thought that they must have their tongues in their cheeks when they spoke of him in such terms. At last I realised that it was his views that caused all this trouble and that they had to believe that Shaw could write his prose and create his Keegans with his tongue in his cheek, for the same reason as their fathers had to believe that the devil in the shape of Shelley could write poetry.

But all this is now changed. With the exception of the few inevitable stragglers Bernard Shaw is now accepted as a person about whom it is necessary to say the correct thing. But, though in the long run his general influence may turn out to be phenomenal, I am convinced that he is still understood and appreciated in the right spirit by remarkably few. For every one man who goes to a Shaw play with the spirit and the understanding also, thousands go only to drown the message and interrupt the poetry by their shrill and damnable laughter – who having seen Heartbreak House protest that 'they enjoyed themselves immensely and laughed all the time'. There is really only one class of people to whom he 'gets across'. Namely, the unsophisticated. They are chiefly found amongst the poorer classes, and it is there that Shaw is better understood than anywhere else – very much better than amongst the theatre-goers. The reception given to the fine but unpretentious *Saint Joan* is interesting in this connection. Few people made the smallest attempt to understand *Back to Methuselah* which is a far greater and more important play than *Saint Joan*, but everyone crowded to the latter loudly insisting that it was his masterpiece. However, it should not be forgotten that there is a third class consisting of men scattered here and there over the country who owe him a debt of gratitude which cannot be expressed by the insult of words.

III

Those who understand Bernard Shaw are few: those who praise him are many. In fact, praise without understanding is beginning to set in with unusual severity even for an accepted literary lion. He has now to face the new danger of losing the little influence he has by becoming a classic. There is a story that he was asked not long ago if the sale of his books was not rather lower than his reputation might lead one to expect. 'Of course it is,' he replied. 'No one reads me at all.' 'Not so bad as that!' protested the other. 'O yes it is,' he answered. 'I'm already a Classic.' The making of a writer a classic is a cunning device by which all men with awkward views are rendered powerless — a sort of Literary House of Lords into which a writer can be kicked up stairs. At first his work is ignored; when it can no longer be ignored it is attacked; when it can no longer be attacked it is praised. That is sufficient. 'Woe unto me when all men praise me!' cries Saint Joan, thus expressing in one colossally dramatic sentence the whole philosophy of Disillusion. Joan the Maid struggling against impossible odds, facing the Trial, entering the Fire could stir and wring the hearts of men: but Joan the Saint has no such influence, and can only be spoken of in the taken-for-granted manner so aptly given to the envoy from Rome in the Epilogue to *Saint Joan*. Jesus of Nazareth preaching in vain, despairing in the garden, but not afraid before Pilate and not flinching from the Cross, could claim to be a light that lighteneth every man who cometh into the world: but Christ the Son of God slopped over with lip-praise by the betrayers of Christianity is an object of indifference. Siddhattha Gautama, the bored aristocrat and turncoat on splendour, soldier for Light and priest of Nirvana, could be hailed indeed during his lifetime as the father of a church and the founder of a faith: but the Buddha of a later date with a golden idol by the altar in the temple at Lhassa, with followers insisting that his birth was celebrated by convulsions in the sky just as the followers of Jesus insisted that his death was announced by the rending of the veil, ceased to be a philosopher and became only the vilest of superstitions. Everyone knows what measures Mahomet took to defend himself after his death against his followers — Mahomet who was as lucky in being followed by Abu Bekr as Jesus was unlucky in being followed by St. Paul. The history of the Saints from the austere Benedict to the lovable Francis of Assisi reveals the same tragedy and implies the same warning against the too faithful follower. Every prophet should have written over his tomb 'Beware of my followers!' For it is not the persecutions of great men by their contemporaries that does harm but the praise they receive from posterity. It was not the Cross that slew Christ, but praise. We have learnt this lesson nowadays, so we no longer stone our prophets when they become dangerous, and therefore useful. We praise them instead.

Thus when we turn to the world of letters we find the same thing. Shelley was driven from University College Oxford: at the present day a hundred yards farther down High Street undergraduates write papers upon him in the Examinations Schools. But that is not because Shelley's type of mind is now appreciated at Oxford, but only because his poetry is recognised while his thoughts are neglected. If he returned again the same fate would be ready for him as certainly as the modern Cross and the modern Fire would be ready for Christ or the Maid. Ibsen is now considered respectable enough to be read (if not hopelessly out of date), but his readers are about as interested in the test-all-things philosophy as were the poisoners of Socrates. Ruskin's case is interesting. Most classics are looked upon as authors whom it is a pleasure to read but unnecessary to understand. Ruskin is looked upon as a good man to read so long as you realise that everything he said was wrong. Thus if you mention Gothic architecture as being the best kind of architecture you are confidently answered by 'Oh, that was only Ruskin's notion' without the slightest attempt to say why he was wrong. The same with Macaulay; it is still done to read him, but only on the understanding that all his facts were wrong and all his views were warped. Carlyle's case, as he said himself, 'hardly bears thinking about'. He was obviously a man of action rather than a man of letters. He would have made, as Frank Harris has pointed out, a magnificent Cromwell. But they wouldn't make any use of him. He told England (Dean Inge has reminded us that it is not too late even now) that if we are going to colonize we must do it properly, i.e. fill Australia, Canada, South Africa with our own people, and thus save perhaps not only our own country but all the world from aggression. But they would not listen to him. They never listened to him. Instead they admired his descriptions of dead men and made him a figure-head: he was allowed to waste and to wither.

We can kill Shaw quite easily in the same way if we want to do so. Already some of his *Plays for Puritans* are being 'done' in schools with the result that boys are gradually being taught to look upon him as an author whom it is necessary to 'do' and get it over as soon as possible. The days of the annotator with his Notes and Appendix are not far off; and the stage will at last be reached when it will be considered safe to set examinations on Mr. Shaw's remarks about examinations.

This recalls a somewhat interesting scene at the end of a lecture Shaw gave in the summer of 1921. A gentleman who up till that hour had taken the tongue-in-his-cheek, music-hall-turn, don't-like-this-brilliant-stuff, view of Bernard Shaw, was so impressed by the lecture that he sprang to his feet and delivered a long speech declaring how at last he believed in Mr. Shaw, and imploring him to make no more jokes in the future but to speak to serious men seriously. Mr. Shaw's reply at the end of the discussion which ensued was what the papers call 'characteristic'. 'Not taking me seriously,' he said, 'is the Englishman's way of refusing to face facts. . . . But I see there is a tendency nowadays to begin treating me like an Archbishop. I fear in that case that I must be becoming a hopeless old twaddler.'

But in spite of all this I am convinced that if Bernard Shaw is understood it does not matter if he is praised. The following pages are just one more effort before it is too late to try and get the public to understand no less than to read him. I, too, will offer praise and blame as I deal with him now as an artist, now as tub-thumper, now as a Tory, now as a mystic, but I warn the reader that however much I may praise him at intervals in this book which insists upon being written, the fact remains that in the future, praise without understanding is a deadly substitute for a little understanding without praise.

CHAPTER THREE
'Gone Out and Gone Wrong'

*

In Mr. Shaw's interesting attack on Mr. Arthur Bingham Walkley in the introduction to *Man and Superman*, he tells us what an intensely refractory person he himself is — 'liable to go out and go wrong at inconvenient moments and with incendiary possibilities'. I submit that nowhere has he so completely and inconveniently gone out and gone wrong as when he was writing *The Revolutionist's Handbook* at the other end of the same volume.

It would not matter if it was just the sudden frenzy of a sensitive soul. But it is a considered treatise and is still referred to by its creator in terms of affection and self-congratulation. Perhaps the oddest thing about it is its title. It looks like a slip of the pen. He calls it *The Revolutionist's Handbook*, but immediately points out that all revolutions are futile because they do nothing but shift the burden of tyranny from one shoulder to another. Our only hope, he tells us, lies in Evolution — and in all respects it is *The Evolutionist's Handbook*. It is impossible not to regard this treatise as Bernard Shaw's one unforgivable sin. The argument is as follows. No well-informed man can contemplate our present civilisation without desiring a change for the better. How are we to bring about such a change? By applying the remedies suggested by certain meliorists; foremost amongst these remedies is a redistribution of wealth (with the necessary corollary of forced labour for the idle). But, insists Mr. Shaw, unhappily man as we know him does not sufficiently desire such progress to bring it about. He desires the end all right but does not sufficiently desire it to take the collective trouble to reach it.

What then are we to do? We must breed a world of supermen. 'As to the method,' says Mr. Shaw, 'what can be said as yet except that where there is a will there is a way.' In short we have not sufficient will to produce the millenium by economic means but there may be a sufficient will to produce it by good breeding. But, as he says himself, there is only one way by which you can get satisfactory results in good breeding – namely, by arranging the basis of society in such a way that anyone can marry anyone else without loss of dignity, instead of sexual selection being confined to classes. But such a basis of society can only come with a proper distribution of wealth. Mr. Shaw therefore says in effect, 'We have not sufficient will to bring about the millenium for its own sake but we have sufficient will to bring it about for the sake of possible supermen.' I do not wish to overdo 'the logical trick' here, but Mr. Shaw has so obscured the argument by his manner of writing, that the above summary of what he says in this treatise, is just.

Therefore the value of *The Revolutionist's Handbook* as a constructive work is negligible. Let us now look at its destructive side – its attack on

Progress. Whatever else it may be, it is certainly a magnificent example of Shaw's method of gathering up facts and hurling them at us as if they were bombs. He must, like Charles Reade, be a man of many notebooks. He must have special columns in which he puts down 'facts concerning cruelty', 'facts concerning treatment of children' and so on as they come before his notice whether through Press, correspondence, observation, conversation, or research. 'All Art is collaboration,' wrote John Synge. Precisely: the collaboration of facts and ideas into an artistic whole. I sometimes think that a genius impresses himself on the world in exact proportion to the degree in which he has managed to capture his passing thoughts and passing facts, put them on an envelope and then transfer them to a notebook. The importance of such a habit can hardly be over-estimated: these thoughts and fruitful facts must be shot at and brought down as they fly by, or else as Samuel Butler insisted they are lost for ever.

The Revolutionist's Handbook as an example of Shavian fact-throwing is very good, but as a treatise on progress it is unconvincing and comes with somewhat of an anti-climax after the play in which that tremendous third act bursts out like a conflagration. Mr. Shaw himself would be the first to admit that we can only decide whether man has progressed or not by measuring his story on the scale of universal history. In the light of universal history we have only lived for a few minutes since Neolithic Man. In tackling the problem of progress we should therefore ask ourselves whether we are an improvement on Neolithic Man and not whether we are an improvement on the Greeks and Latins.

This is commonplace, a platitude I hope by this time. Yet what are we to make of Mr. Shaw's outburst: 'Parliaments and vestries are just what they were when Cromwell suppressed them and Dickens derided them. The democratic politician remains exactly as Plato described him; the physician is still the incredulous impostor and petulant scientific coxcomb whom Molière ridiculed; the schoolmaster remains at best a pedantic child farmer and at worst a flagellomaniac'? One wonders what the writer would wish to prove by comparing the Parliaments of to-day with the Parliaments of yesterday. The gentlemen who talk about Shaw as a man with his tongue in his cheek can at least quote this Handbook in defence. Those who understand Mr. Shaw are forced to look upon it as a result of one of those moments (perhaps not altogether regrettable) when he has gone out and gone wrong with incendiary possibilities.

Again, he says 'Man as we know him will not improve' – as if human nature (if it existed) was a stationary thing. How the author of *Back to Methuselah* could make such a meaningless statement is a dark mystery. What is the great lesson that Evolution teaches us? What is the great corollary that we must draw from the knowledge that we are descended and therefore have ascended from jellyfish? Simply that there is no such thing as human nature.

There is no such thing as human nature. If we once admit that we are not separate creations it follows that no line can be drawn between us and the animals. Indeed it is the essence of this world that no lines can ever be drawn anywhere. This especially applies to the evolution of life. There was no definite point when the walking ape ceased to be a walking ape and became a man. All an Unseen Watcher could have said was 'I have seen a grim hairy creature intent on its food and its family with little other brain work; and then later I have seen the same creature greatly altered, its lips sometimes breaking to let forth a new noise called laughter, and its brain more developed. So altered in fact that I will call it "Man".' He would no doubt admit that if the creature's brain and body had changed its nature had also changed accordingly. But he would not say the first was 'animal nature' and the second 'human nature'. If he wanted to put an adjective before the word 'nature' he would say that the first was ape nature and the second man nature. And he would recognise that as man's body and brain gradually changed more so also would his nature change more.

Unhappily owing to our conceit and to the

religion which we invented to accord with that conceit we have up till the nineteenth century placed ourselves on a pedestal and proclaimed that the Creator instead of slowly evolving us from lower species, specially created us as we now are. Forgetting that nature does nothing but change, we called ourselves *human beings* and proclaimed that human nature never changes — the adjective *human*, observe, acting merely as a pious prefix to the nature of wonderful man. We even went so far as to give particulars and say that God had made us in His own image instead of recognising the fact that we had made God in our own image. We believed that we alone possessed souls — the animals apparently being soulless. And finally we held it as a proper arrangement that we alone would live for ever in another world later on. We experienced no more difficulty in believing these things than in believing the frightful lie told to us as children that God had suddenly invented languages to spite the builders of Babel even though it practically meant periodical war in which His creatures would destroy themselves.

Well, all this has been changed by the Evolutionists. God is not dead. But an important chapter in the history of God has been reached. He is no longer in the sky, no longer omnipotent, no longer a monster.

Unfortunately though the average man appears to be now either an atheist or a Creative Evolutionist, he still seems to consider man as something very special. He believes that man's nature never changes. What an article of faith! What a comment that faith is upon his whole outlook on the past, the present and the future! What appalling conceit, what shameless complacency! Let us be humble. Let us at least be logical in this matter. Then we can march prospering – but not through such nonsense. It was right for our ancestors who knew not Darwin to talk about 'human' nature. It is right for the muddle-headed to feel ashamed at being descended from monkeys instead of proud at having ascended from them. It is right for the Roman Catholic, gallantly fighting against Truth, to exalt Man above all other creatures on the earth. But how can we, who know that even the least of the animals can claim our brotherhood, talk about nature as if it was either special or immutable?

God threw Satan from Paradise. To-day the heavens are empty, for He himself has fallen. Let Man fall from his pedestal also – a Fall of Man which will mean something! Not until then can we march forward again rejoicing in the real God whom we know to be within us and whom we feel to be behind us.

What, it may be asked, is my exact complaint against Shaw? Simply that he says 'unfortunately all the earnest people get drawn off the track of evolution by the illusion of progress'. But what is the difference? No one can seriously suppose that if man was a stationary non-evolving species, his affairs would reach perfection of organisation. But when we see that he *is* an evolving creature how can we help believing in progress? There can be no progress that is not also anatomical — though of course the changed body is only the reflection of the changed mind. We can believe, though we cannot prove, that Life is always changing for the better, that our characters are getting more god-like. All life is one. When I was a jellyfish I thought as a jellyfish, but now that I am a man I think as a man — and I hold it as an article of faith that I think better. Our thoughts are what ultimately matter: and I believe that as a jellyfish I thought better than as an amœba, that as a reptile I thought better than as a jellyfish, that as a monkey I thought better than as a reptile, and that as a man I think better than as a monkey. This may be mere conceit: but it is a reasonable conceit: it is a noble conceit. It gives me hope. I can believe that if I am now better than I was as a Walking Ape a hundred thousand years ago, so will I be better than I am now after another hundred thousand years have passed — for there is surely no reason to suppose that the Force that made Life will suddenly pause in astonishment at Man's perfection and cry a halt! I can look forward to the time when immediate life will be worth living and our fellows worth loving. No doubt before that time comes we may have a large number of wars and revolutions and rises and falls of civilisations. But that does not matter. Life is cheap, Death is harmless, Time is long. We will go on evolving all the same — for revolution cannot stop evolution. It is nonsense to say that we may exterminate one another in the meantime. All the women must be killed first: and we may count it as fairly certain that that will never happen.

That is what I will venture to call Progress — the eternal progression and unassailable ascension of the Holy Ghost. Otherwise the word can have no meaning. For as man evolves into something higher he will become increasingly able to overcome his economic difficulties. As a Bible for such Progress Mr. Shaw has offered us *Back to Methuselah*.

That brings me to Superman. Here again Mr. Shaw is always confusing us. He advocates the Superman. He pleads for conferences to consult how best to breed Supermen out of ourselves. He offers us Supermen in the shape of Ancients. Yet he never loses an opportunity of warning us against being superseded by creatures higher than ourselves.

But surely there can be no doubt that the superman will evolve out of us. We are the most conscious of the animals. And consciousness is surely what the Life Force is looking for rather than anything else. But even supposing the Superman was to try and evolve out of the flea or the giraffe, would we tolerate them? We command the earth: we are jealous creatures: we are specialists in death and destruction. Who can doubt that if the Superman were seen evolving from giraffes (his neck being used as a watch-tower instead of as a biological example of natural selection) we would immediately turn from the pursuits of homicide to the business of destroying these new enemies?

If we once accept the fact that we are not a separate creation it is surely absurd to suppose that we are either the last or the best creation. If the Life Force has gone as far as us it is extremely unlikely that it will stop with us. We should not be afraid of the coming of the Supermen. Rather should we rejoice at their possible advent and do all we can to bring it about.

The fact that the sun may be cooling and the earth dying should not be taken into consideration. It is useless for Dean Inge to tell us that the best thing we can do is to sit down quietly and firmly and watch the sun cooling. It is useless for Mr. Bertrand Russell to tell us to base all our philosophy upon that basis. It is useless for Anatole France to paint a picture of man returning to the caves even as he emerged from them. It is useless for Mr. H. G. Wells to tell us in one part of his *Outline of History* that the sun is cooling and in another that it is not. The fact remains that there is no proof whatever that the future of Life is necessarily dependent either upon the earth or on the sun's rays. I do not say that interplanetary communication is the answer to these things – hopping from planet to planet would not necessarily get us away from the final problem – but I do say that for us to despair because the sun may be cooling (though even that is now contradicted I understand) is no more sensible than it was for the Diplodocus to despair of life advancing farther than the marshes. It is surely better – not to say more healthy – to take Shaw's attitude in this matter and realise that at present it is quite impossible to tell what Life may yet do in defiance of Suns and Earths and all kinds of Matter. It is far wiser to say with Shaw (who does not measure his scepticism) that a man should have enough sense of humour to prevent him from believing that the sun which is so near to us that a cloud can make the difference between hot and cold, is ninety-three million miles away, than to sit down with Dean Inge to watch it cool.

Mr. Shaw realises much clearer than most of us the absurdity of the current talk about human nature never changing. He has written *Back to Methuselah* to show that there is one thing we definitely do know, namely that Life is always changing, and that therefore human life (or better, Man Life) is no more proof against change than was Diplodocus life. Further, he has written that great play – as I will again point out when dealing with his characterisation – to expose the foul mockery of the assumption that the business of a dramatist is merely to hold the mirror up to man as he is and never to man as he may become.

It is regrettable that the dramatist who has done us this service should also be proud of having written a treatise on a quibble and then miscalled it the Revolutionist's Handbook.

CHAPTER FOUR

Divination: God: The Divinity that Shapes our Ends:
Shaw's Message to Normal Man

★

I

I ONCE asked Mr. Shaw why he ate cabbages if he would not eat flesh, since no line can logically be drawn between a vegetable (merely a dumb creature) and an animal. . . . 'Stop talking logic to me,' he said, 'you cannot apply logic to everything.'[1] Though Mr. Shaw pursues most terrestrial arguments to their logical conclusion with the same Irish ruthlessness that forced John McSwiney to starve in an English gaol and Mary McSwiney to try and do so in an Irish one, he nevertheless is no logician. Nor is he a reasonable man — 'he who listens to Reason is lost: Reason enslaves all those whose minds are not strong enough to master her.' His faith lies in divination.

That should not surprise this age. It was only for a short period that men regarded themselves as reasonable creatures and women as unreason-

[1] He added — 'Vegetarian diet is for poets and philosophers, meat for the rest if you like. Moreover, we must get rid of our dependence upon animals. We are valets to the cow, the goat, and the sheep. Go into a place where dogs are kept and look at the faces of the animals' servants, and you will find them more dog-like than the dogs themselves. And by the way,' he continued, 'don't stick simply a dish of cabbages in front of the vegetarian — for that is not the only vegetarian dish!'

able — and therefore unreliable — ones. We have learnt now to trust more in divination than in reason and logic — perhaps that is why women have been given the vote. Anyway, Mr. Shaw's position as a biologist will never be appreciated until we realise that the divination part of him is more important than any other part.

He is fond of reminding us that the inspired prophet jumps across the facts to the conclusion — facts which later on are produced by less inspired scientists — Blake said the same thing in a different way — 'What is now proved was once only imagined'. Mr. Shaw's voice comes clearly through the words of Joan: 'I always give you reasons for the things I tell you to do. But I never think of the reasons till afterwards.' That applies very strongly to his own case. When he was a very young man he held views upon vivisection, medicine, meat-eating, prisons, punishment, marriage, God, Darwinism and many other subjects which he has seldom modified with advancing years. All his biggest ideas can be found in embryo in his novels and his early works like *The Quintessence of Ibsenism* and *The Perfect Wagnerite*. It was not till years afterwards that he produced reasons for his various articles of faith. In fact there is something almost sinister about his mind as a young man. He did not slowly fight out a philosophy and religion like Wells. He was born a mystic. The result of this on his work is very obvious and very edifying. It stands firm as if upon a rock so that the reader is never in any fear of being suddenly let down. It has been the custom to talk a great deal about the number of Mr. Shaw's ideas. But that is Wells' quality not Shaw's. The distinctive mark of Shaw's work is the way in which he delivers a select number of ideas all pointing in the same direction. That is why, with the exception of *The Revolutionist's Handbook*, there are no blind alleys in his work. All his plays are one long cycle in which he again and again proclaims his faith that every man is a Man of Destiny, a Servant of the Life Force, and a Temple of the Holy Ghost.

Owing to insufficiency of knowledge I can make no criticism of Mr. Shaw's criticism of Neo-Darwinianism. But this I will say: it would be unwise not to listen with considerable attention to the attacks on pseudo-science by a man who speaks with such obvious inspiration as Mr. Shaw, in an age like this which has taught us to appreciate Seneca's words 'we imagine that we are initiated into the mysteries of Nature; but we are still hanging about her outer courts'.

Mysticism and divination are abstractions hard to write about in prose; but that must not blind us to the fact that Shaw the Mystic is more important than Shaw the political analyst and that the things he divines are more important than the things he proves. For instance the fact that he divined *Candida* before he found out the whole truth about it (as he says) is of enormous importance.

II

The danger of taking a superficial view of Bernard Shaw may perhaps be illustrated by the following remark which I heard him make. He was speaking to a group of young men asking questions. It was of Dean Inge that he spoke — '. . . . But I like him. . . . I suppose it is because he has the same religion as myself.'

Let us briefly state Shaw's well-known conception of God. Behind the Universe there is a vague power which we may call the Life Force. About the origin of this Power we know nothing. It is neither all-powerful nor all-knowing, but it is striving to become both by means of its own creations. It goes forward by the process of trial and error. The last trial so far is Man. He may also be an error. But he is not a 'base accident of nature'.

That in short is Shaw's God. He does not strike Dean Inge's fancy. Writing of those who believe in such a God he says: 'according to these apologists God seems to make a poor job of governing the world; we can only say of Him with Dr. McTaggart that He is "on the whole good rather than bad" — a restricted testimonial which would hardly procure an engagement for a housemaid except under post-war conditions.' Why then does Shaw declare that the Dean holds the same religion as himself? The answer is that both are mystics and that they join together in their mysticism. They both hold the same ultimate values concerning 'the Good, the True, and the Beautiful'. But I mention Shaw's remark only to show that he has a real respect for any man who is genuinely religious though his God may not be quite the same as his own. He is probably one of the very few persons in England who understands what Inge means by saying 'it is not always that I can pray with the spirit and the understanding also; which is a very different thing from simply "saying one's prayers" ' – for it is a mistake to think that Bernard Shaw never prays. He does – in an empty Church.[1]

But returning to Shaw's actual God, does He not compare very favourably with many other conceptions of God? (I use the term God at intervals throughout this book meaning in Shaw's case the Life Force. I do so because I happen to like the word.) Is the Life Force not an improvement on Wells' Nature – that 'wretched hag of whom mankind is but the last child of her wantonings!'?

---

[1] I do not know how far the Dean feels spiritually akin to Shaw. A short time after Shaw made that remark I happened to be debating with the Dean at the Oxford Union on the subject of Victorianism. I asked him afterwards how he thought Shaw compared with the great Victorians about whom he had been talking. 'Oh,' he replied, 'he is very difficult to place . . . he has still (referring to *Back to Methuselah*) plenty of the old fire left. But he is so dreadfully irresponsible. However, I like him better than – – and – –!'

on Bertrand Russell's accidental atoms? on the God of the Old Testament who, in a fit of pique, gave His creations the scourge of languages and commanded Saul to slay and spare not? Shaw's God of Creative Evolution is the only God that answers the problem of evil. For the great point about Darwin's *Origin of Species* is that it does *not* explain the origin of species but *does* explain the origin of evil.

III

But the difficult part about Mr. Shaw's Life Force has yet to be stated. He is often accused of being a Calvinist. It is an accusation that at first seems just. He is always telling us that Shakespeare's phrase 'there is a divinity which shapes our ends rough hew them how we will' is the statement of a scientific fact. What else does that mean but that there is a power behind us which governs our lives no matter what we do? And what else is that but Calvinism, or at any rate Calvinism without Tears? Then if we turn to the plays we find that most of the characters from Undershaft to Blanco Posnet acknowledge that they acted under the influence of a power over which they had no final control.

In order to try and clear this up I put the question direct to him one evening at a meeting. His reply in effect was 'You misunderstand me: I am not a Calvinist. It is true I wrote Blanco Posnet out of that phrase of Shakespeare's, but he rough hewed his way very considerably before he acted to the power outside him. The power was also inside him.' The reader must make what he can out of that reply, but whatever he makes of it he will I am confident eventually come to see that there is an enormous difference between Shaw's view and the fatalistic personal God of Calvin who arranges not only each man's actions in this world but his dwelling-place hereafter.

Shaw postulates a General Life Force behind everything – which gives everyone an Individual Driving Force. This Driving Force or Divinity is as yet in a very primitive condition. Like the General Life Force it is sometimes good, sometimes foolish, sometimes wholly evil. It may shape the destiny of some inspired brigand like Napoleon, or some murderer like Crippen. It may serve the interests of nationalism like Joan of Arc, the interests of knowledge like Lamarck, or the interests of religion like Jesus. In each case the individual is driven forward by a power greater than himself. Each individual may rough hew his destiny as much as he will but he cannot get away from the Driving Force within him, and so it is 'up to him' to turn it to noble rather than ignoble ends. What is the test of a noble action? Blanco Posnet replies that if you do the wrong thing you have a 'a rotten feel', and if you do the right thing you 'lose the rotten feel'.

Does Shaw postulate that one person has more Divinity driving him on than another? Decidedly.

The Driving Power of an individual must range as much as the horse-power of different motors. Perhaps the doctors of the future will be able to test the exact amount of a person's Divinity as easily as they now can test his pulse. Thus if we see a great many Napoleons and Crippens going about we can rejoice because we know Divinity (let us not confuse that word with the Sunday-school meaning) is strong within them. We should hold as an article of Faith that the time will come when all Divinity will make for righteousness just as the time will come when the General Life Force will have attained complete power.

IV

What then is Bernard Shaw's message to normal men? What is his message to people who are not murderers, who are not generals, who are not founders of religions, people who seem to have no particular flair at all? What is his message to the man on the bus, to the stockbroker, to the tailor, to the thousands who toil only that they may live and live only that they may toil, to the mothers of sorrow and daughters of toil and suffering who make up our world? For after all the realities of life have little to do with Napoleons and Saint Joans and such like. Indeed it is impossible to look at the pictures in a magazine or go to the cinema without feeling with a sort of shock how plain life has become, how cowardly, mean and unlovely we all must be if we insist that these pictures must in all things and in every instance avoid the smallest semblance to reality.

What then is Bernard Shaw's message to normal men? It is merely that they should cease to be normal men. To all those who ask with the Dauphin in *Saint Joan*, 'Why don't the voices come to *me*?' he replies through the lips of the Maid, 'They do come to you but you do not hear them.' He does not of course mean real voices but promptings of the spirit, which cannot come to us so long as we remain as we are 'blind and deaf to the calls and visions of the inexorable power that made us and will destroy us if we disregard it'.

CHAPTER FIVE

The Builder: The Immoralist: The Tory

*

I

It has become the fashion to speak of Shaw as a consistent but destructive writer. The truth is that consistency is by no means his strong point, while steady constructive criticism on most subjects is a notable characteristic of his work.

He is not consistent in *Back to Methuselah*, for in Act III the burden of long living is given to people who have not desired to live longer; long life is thrust upon them by some unseen power — which is contrary to the teaching of the Preface. He is not consistent on the subject of progress — as I have endeavoured to show. He is not consistent on the subject of Money, for in public speeches he often gives the lie to Undershaft and dramatically confronts him with Shotover. He is not consistent on the subject of sex, for he hints twice in *Heartbreak House* that children are lovely in proportion to the love of the parents for each other, but elsewhere advocates the old maid's right to motherhood, in which love does not come into it. He is not consistent on the subject of work, for he often insists that you should work to the point of wearing your health out, while in the Preface to *Misalliance* he joins with Herbert Spencer in warning us against overwork as against drink — not to mention his pretence about his working for only two hours a day when he obviously works for eighteen! He is not consistent on the subject of liberty if we compare his final remarks in the Preface to *Misalliance* with his frequent denunciation of liberty elsewhere. I hasten to admit that often the inconsistency is only on the surface and that he clings with remarkable fidelity to certain main themes, never swerving from them for an instant. But if a little less was said about his consistency there would be more chance of clearing up all his inconsistencies.

But nothing can militate more against a proper understanding of Bernard Shaw than to imagine that he is a destructive writer. Nothing could be less true. Of course he indulges in plenty of destruction as well as construction, for it must be remembered that to be a master-builder you must also be a master-destroyer, and that 'for every sanctuary that is erected a sanctuary must be pulled down.' Shaw appears to be very destructive simply because he is very constructive. But there are some people who always notice destruction but never construction just as there are some who always hear the voice of Larry Doyle but never the voice of Keegan.

If in the Preface to *Getting Married* he has attacked the divorce laws he has not failed to suggest what should be done to make marriage a healthy institution. If in the Preface to *Major Barbara* he has attacked the Salvation Army he has not failed to raise it to a position of dignity unthought of before. If in the Preface to *John Bull's Other Island* he laid bare the souls of both Islands he nevertheless made such a clear exposition of the Irish situation as to wring from Mr. Devlin the acknowledgment that 'Shaw has stated the Irish Question once and for all'. If in *The Doctor's Dilemma* he has attacked the position of the Medical Profession he has not attacked Medicine but has made many valuable suggestions such as his advocation of Dr. Saleeby's Sun Cure with its necessary slogan of Back to Hippocrates – (but his advocation of this sovereign cure of sunshine was greeted by the gentlemen who accused him of destruction, as pure moonshine!) If in the Preface to *Misalliance* he is wholly destructive it is because, as will follow from what I will say in the next chapter, he is wholly constructive in his views about children. If in the Preface to *Back to Methuselah* he has attacked the Neo-Darwinians he has not failed to offer Creative Evolution in place of their teaching. If in his Preface to Mr. and Mrs. Sidney Webb's book on Prisons he has attacked prisons tooth and nail he has not failed to go into elaborate details as to how we should deal with malefactors. If he is purely destructive upon the subject of vivisection, flogging, and such like, it is because he wishes to destroy them for ever.

I am deliberately labouring this point because when we consider the wealth of miscellaneous construction there is to be found in his Prefaces, the wealth of Political construction to be found in his *Hints for the Peace Conference, Fabian Essays, Common-sense of Municipal Trading* and so on, the wealth of Religious construction to be found in such works as *The Sanity of Art*, *The Perfect Wagnerite*, *The Quintessence of Ibsenism*, or the forewords to his novels, and finally when we consider how the Plays themselves make up the various books in a Bible of Evolution, it is difficult to refrain from coming to the conclusion that he is one of the most constructive writers who have ever lived.

II

Nevertheless there is a distinct topsy-turveyism about all his work which certainly gives the impression of singularity for the sake of singularity — until we look closer. The most important thing about Bernard Shaw — more important perhaps even than his mysticism — is that he is not a moralist but a natural historian. When once the significance of that distinction is grasped then all his views, whether we agree with them or not, become perfectly easy to understand.

All his work becomes perfectly straightforward if we choose to follow it in the light of the following two remarks. 'To me the tragedy and comedy of life,' he writes at the end of the Preface to *Plays Pleasant*, 'lie in the consequences sometimes terrible, sometimes ludicrous, of our persistent attempts to found our institutions on the ideals suggested to our imaginations by our half-satisfied passions, instead of on a genuinely scientific natural history. And with that hint as to what I

am driving at I withdraw and ring up the curtain.'
In a letter to H. N. Hyndman appears the following passage (the whole letter being of great interest and vital importance): 'I am a moral revolutionary, interested, not in class war, but in the struggle between human vitality and the artificial system of morality, and distinguishing not between capitalist and proletarian, but between moralist and natural-historian.' If the reader has been interested enough to get as far as this page it will be worth his while to read both the above quotations a large number of times, say, a dozen – for I venture to think that it takes more than one reading to grasp the point he is driving at.

What does he mean by these two declarations? He means that he believes in Growth. He means that he believes in the ultimate success of the Life Force. What he seems to say to us is this: You believe that the world is divided up into good men and bad men, heroes and villains, and therefore you place a system of morality upon them: those who obey that system are moral, those who do not are immoral. You found your education upon this system with the result that a child's mind has to obey the morality instead of its conscience. You base your religious institutions upon the same foundations so that dogmas are formed which defy the law of change. You go out against your political opponents believing that one particular class is in a state of grace and another in a state of sin – and so you get class war. You found your institution of marriage on what you imagine it ought to be and are disappointed at the reality. Now I do not take this view. I do not believe that the world is divided into good and bad men, heroes and villains and the like: Hell is paved with good intentions not with bad ones. I feel no bitterness against the Capitalist, for I know that he is no worse than anyone else. It is natural for him to do as he is doing. I believe in growth by the help of the Life Force. Do not strangle this Vitality in artificial bonds of Morality. Do not moralise to a child: let its conscience teach it. Let your religion grow as thought grows. Do not attack political opponents as if they were bad men: try and make everyone socialistically minded — for only then can we have a social state of things.

That is Shaw the Immoralist. He wishes everyone and anyone to advocate and preach in free open controversy what they like, but he insists that it shall all be done without bitterness and without calling the other fellow immoral. To him morality is only a swear-word. The only morality he recognises is the Conscience, and he advocates that we should obey our conscience and not a ready-made morality. He is probably the most violent opponent of moralising and righteous indignation that the world has ever produced. 'Mere morality,' he writes in the one-page Preface to Fanny's First Play, 'or the substitution of custom for conscience, was once accounted a shameful and cynical thing: people talked of right and wrong, of honour and dishonour, of sin and grace, of salvation and damnation, not of morality and immorality. The word morality, if we met it in the Bible, would surprise us as much as the word telephone or motor-car.' He does not say to a person who asks Shall I do this wicked thing? No, Morality forbids it. He says Yes, if your conscience allows you. Only thus can you get to know yourself and to know what is right and wrong. For your conscience is the Holy Ghost within you. It knows better than systems of morality what is right and wrong. That is what he means when in *The Sanity of Art* he emphasises the widsom of the Eleventh Verse in the Twenty-Second Chapter of Revelations – He that is unjust let him be unjust still: and he which is filthy let him be filthy still: and he that is righteous let him be righteous still: and he that is holy let him be holy still.

What is at the bottom of all Shaw's teaching and attacks upon everything? Why does his cry appear to be, Whatever is, is wrong? Why, though a socialist, has he no patience with Karl Marx and the Class War? The fact is that he happens to believe in his Religion. He believes in Growth. He believes in the innate righteousness and ultimate triumph of what he calls the Life Force (though he does not pretend to know what the Life Force is). He believes in Conscience prompted by the Life Force. He knows that

Conscience is a far harder task-master than morality, and is therefore naturally shirked by the weak. The weak turn away in terror from the asceticism of this man, from his fastidiousness, from his chasteness, from a character so saintly as to make it impossible for even the dirtiest newspaper to breathe a word of scandal against him. Shaw does not address himself to the weak. I suppose his teaching tends to weaken the weaklings no less than to strengthen the strong.

III

There is one more point about Shaw's politics that ought to be cleared up, namely, his Toryism. He was once a democrat. He believed in the people. He rushed madly for twelve years from meeting to meeting to preach socialism. His energy in those early Fabian days is appalling even to read about. He believed that a clear exposition of the economic situation had only got to be put before the people to make them rise up as one man and demand Socialism. He put it before them. What was the result? They agreed with what he said and loudly applauded him — and went home. They did not intend to do anything. They were far too busy living to find time to consider the problem of how they ought to live.

So at length Shaw perceived that Democracy was impossible if it meant not only Government of the people and for the people but *by* the people. He perceived that it was useless to wait till the majority was converted for they never would be converted, and that it was as ridiculous to expect the ordinary man to frame laws for himself as to write plays for himself – and said so. He changed his views and took the point of view that the select minority must force the majority to do its will. That is Toryism à la Ruskin and Carlyle and all true Tories. So Shaw became a Tory. He then perceived that unless the select minority *does* force the majority to do its will things will remain in a state of democratic chaos. That is Bolshevism à la Lenin and Trotsky and all true Bolshevists. So he became a Bolshevist. It must always be remembered that Toryism and Bolshevism are the same thing in the first sense, and that in that sense Baldwin is a Bolshevist and Trotsky a Tory. That is why both Liberals and mild Labour men so bitterly hate Toryism on the one hand and Communism on the other, for they know in their hearts that they are but wanderers in the middle mist falsely pretending to believe in the people.

The point to grasp about the modern Shaw is that, while taking the Tory view of the hopelessness of Democracy, he insists that the minority (not a dictator like Mussolini but a group) must force the majority at the point of the bayonet to do what they (the minority) consider for the good of the state. The first thing he would force is work for all. The reason why we never hear him denouncing the Capitalist is because he knows that if everyone was forced to work by a strong Government all the evils of the Capitalist system would immediately and completely disappear.

But it must be emphasised that this is the least important aspect of Bernard Shaw. Over against these practical suggestions as to the changing of our environment he has expressed his conviction in *Methuselah* that no real progress can come about except it come from *within*. The thing to grasp about Shaw's work as a whole is this: half of it is devoted to saying that much good can be done by Act of Parliament and the other half to saying that Parliaments are the mere reflections of our state of mind and that nothing genuine can be done until our state of mind improves. It is this latter conviction which is the most important and therefore the most neglected – for it is so much more pleasant to abuse our politicians than to abuse ourselves.

CHAPTER SIX

Shavian Education

*

A SHORT time ago Mr. Shaw publicly declared that he was of the opinion that no one should start his education until he is thirty or forty years of age. To a generation that is startled by the audacity of Mr. R. H. Tawney's suggestion that children should not be allowed to become industrial fodder until they are sixteen, such a statement must sound like the ravings of a broken-down schoolmaster. Yet I am convinced that even if we were to suppose that all else Mr. Shaw has ever advocated be false and feigned and foolish that one declaration is triumphantly right.

It explains in a sentence Shaw's whole position as regards education. There can be no doubt whatever that in this matter he still stands practically alone with none so poor to do him reverence. It is not apparent to the average reader and observer of Shaw why he always adopts a certain expression when the word 'professor' is mentioned, why he always refuses to go and speak at Oxford, why he is always ready to back up economy in education, why he does not, with the rest of our educational apologists, throw his school ideals into the future, and why instead of joining in the chorus of 'Secondary Education for All' violently shouts 'Civilisation is being visibly wrecked by educated men; and yet with a hideous infatuation, we seek to cure ourselves by a hair of the dog that bit us, clamouring for more education instead of razing Eton, Harrow, Winchester, Oxford, Cambridge, and the rest of them to the ground, and sowing their sites with salt rather than with dragon's teeth'.

The point is that his whole view of education as the natural pursuit of knowledge is totally different from that held by anyone else. It can be understood best perhaps by those who have much ability but were not successes at school or college. Our schools and universities are always packed with precocious and clever boys who receive all sorts of 'honours' to the mingled contempt and awe of the other boys and to the delight of their proud parents. Then once every generation the world asks with Mr. Ian Hay in his *Lighter Side of School Life*, What becomes of them? Where do they go? And there is a dead silence: for no one knows. If the inevitable exceptions are allowed for, it is safe to say that most of them are tired out by the time they leave educational institutions, and so do not realise that they have reached the age when they ought to start educating themselves properly. They are worn out by the machine of forced learning – that grim engine at the door of life which having smote once need smite no more! 'For though here and there a Lord Macaulay may escape from school honours with all his wits about him,' as R. L. Stevenson wrote in his *Defence of Idlers*, 'most boys pay so dear for their medals that they never afterwards have a shot in their locker, and begin the world bankrupt.'

It is a great mistake for a young man of, say, twenty-four, to feel that he ought to have read a great deal. 'Heavens, how awfully ill-read I am!' he may say to himself, 'I haven't read nearly as much as So-and-so. I haven't even read Darwin's *Origin of Species*, though I should have read all such books long ago.' The fact is if he has not read many of the epoch-making books of the world before he is twenty-four he is exceedingly lucky. If he has read them he is exceedingly unlucky. For consider what happens in the cases of the precocious and unprecocious boy (using the term 'boy' for both sexes). Supposing the precocious boy has read *The Origin of Species* when he was in his teens, what is the result? He has read it, that is all. He can point to the shelf and say 'I have read *The Origin of Species*'. It is on the shelf of his mind so to say. A hundred to one he remembers nothing of it and has gained nothing from it other than the bare fact that we are descended from monkeys – if that for Darwin does not actually mention the fact. If on the other hand he has allowed his mind to mature for about twenty-four years and then tackles the epochmaking books, the result is very profitable. The books suggest all sorts of things to his mind which would never have struck him if he had read them earlier. They give him visions of life instead of merely being additions to the number of books he has read.

It must not be thought that I wish to imply that books are the only things that educate a person.

Far from it. Who does not agree with Cashel Byron that it would be a grand thing to meet an educated person who had never read anything? And probably most musicians would endorse Mr. Shaw's contention that 'it is possible to learn more of the world by producing a single opera, or even conducting a single orchestral rehearsal, than by ten years' reading in the library of the British Museum'. And the average doctor – notoriously ill-read – must know more about contemporary men, since life is daily laid naked at his feet, than almost any of his fellows: not that that is everything. Nevertheless in passing I would defend myself as a person who reads books against the person who declaims against reading. We all know the worthy 'good fellow' who says to one so charmingly, 'I don't believe in too much reading you know. Read men, don't read books. . . .' Such people are apt to forget that to many men – I do not say to all men – reading is *learning*: learning of the past so as to understand the present and to foretell the future, learning facts to use as bombs in the battle of life. A man may say 'I don't like reading' and be thought a fine fellow for saying so; but if he really was a fine fellow he would say what he means – 'I don't like *learning*'. And it is right to add that the person who 'doesn't read many books' is seldom found on inspection to 'read many men'.

But Mr. Shaw goes much further than saying that a man should not read important books until he is twenty-four. He suggests the figures thirty or forty. And he urges that a person should have no schooling at all either before or after that age. He realises that schools are merely developments out of the failure of the family — a fact which I notice is proved by the letters mothers write to the papers every time a school breaks-up early. He replies now as always to the grim lady who rises from the back of the lecture hall to ask — 'Mr. Shaw has advocated the abolition of schools. What will be put in their place?' 'I will put nothing in their place. Schools are prisons. I was in prison, etc., etc.!' He urges that the child's mind should be allowed as much freedom to develop as the flowers in the field except that it should learn enough arithmetic and reading to prevent it from being a nuisance to other people. It need hardly be said that if arithmetic and reading gave the privilege of extra freedom to those who learnt them, then the pursuit of arithmetic and reading would be more enthusiastic than the pursuit of Arabian Treasures.

Why does Shaw take up this attitude towards children? Why does he advocate things which are clearly impossible until our present system of economic slavery and personal danger are things of the past? Well, again I must state that the trouble with Shaw simply is that he happens to believe in his religion. He believes that there is an Energy behind every child pressing it forward in an experimental way. He believes that this

Energy or Life Force has tried with the Brontosaurus and Diplodocus to see what bodily strength could do, with birds to see what beauty could do, with bees and such-like to see what Instinct could do, and finally with man to see what Brains could do. He believes that this Life Force having evolved Brains and therefore Consciousness will soon evolve super-brains and super-consciousness. He believes that when we are super-conscious we will know what Life is. He believes, I repeat, in this God of his, and he will not suffer the ignorant and the unreflecting, the stupid and the bloody-minded, the coarse and the base-thinking to take hold of children, to cram them into a building and pour cataracts of pseudo-knowledge upon them, to surround them with moral man-made laws, to soak them in traditions, to bathe them with dogmas, to blind them with superstitions, and in every way to disallow their real instincts and to suppress their real thoughts. Nor does he look with much greater favour upon the high-minded and the well-gifted who believe that they know what is good for children so much better than God.

Thus if we look through Shaw's work we will discover that nowhere is he more serious and nowhere does he write with more beauty or vigour than when dealing with the subject of children — his Preface to *Misalliance* has given strength and courage to thousands whose early days have been embittered by savage schoolmasters or twisted by poisonous mothers. It is with no surprise that we find him, in a letter to a friend, speaking of the Preface in the language of passion – 'The tears of countless children have fallen unavenged. I will turn them into boiling vitriol and force it into the souls of their screaming oppressors!'

CHAPTER SEVEN

No 'real' Bernard Shaw: The Sword that Slew the
Slayer: Parnassus: On the Platform

♣

I

IN a sense Bernard Shaw is one of the most real men who have ever lived. Real, that is to say, in so far as he has always striven to be himself, to express himself, and to be true to himself. There is nothing artificial about him. But in a less profound sense he consists of a large number of persons, and therefore it is exceedingly hard at any given moment to find the real man.

The truth is there seldom is a 'real' anybody. At regular intervals books come out which are reviewed as giving 'the real Robert Louis Stevenson at last'. We are told frequently that only by reading the letters of So-and-so can we find 'the real man'. Critics fasten on a certain book of an author and protest that in that book 'he reveals himself'. In each case it is assumed that the author in question consists of one person especially who up to that time has managed to conceal himself from the public.

It never will be possible to understand a genius — specially in the case of Bernard Shaw — so long as this view is taken. It is impossible to find 'the real man' because he does not exist. Every man (especially great men) are composed of a number of different persons who may like or dislike each other, who may work together in harmony or keep tripping over one another, but who have nothing in common save the house of flesh they live in. It has puzzled some persons why Turner, who walked with Nature in spirit and in truth when he was at work, immediately it was over became a mere animal slobbering in the pubs at Rotherhithe; why Sir James Barrie so continuously splits himself up, as completely as lesser men split an apple, into Macconachy and The Other Half; why Mr. A. E. Housman is a walking repudiation of the author of *The Shropshire Lad*; why Dean Inge can tell us again and again that miners ought to be less well-off than himself and yet remain the gentlest and most Christian of our modern leaders. But there is nothing in the least surprising in any of the contradictions when we remember that we are all composed of several persons. No man lets his left hand know what his right hand doeth. Every man with the dramatic instinct continually stands aghast at the lack of control he has over his different selves – 'to think that half an hour ago I was that person and now I am this person!' is his continual exclamation. And in passing, as regards letter writing, I will venture to say that it is ridiculous to suggest that an author's letters to his friends are any more real than his public work. They represent one part of him, that is all. Often they represent a very unimportant part of him, for many authors like Pope write letters hoping to have them published surreptitiously 'without the author's permission', while nearly every other author who can write a letter writes (though he does not know it) with an eye to posterity. No, if a man's letters can help you to understand him more than superficially, I submit that they are not his letters to his friends, not his letters to his wife, not his letters to his family, but his letters at moments of political crisis to the daily papers.

A great man is successful (perhaps I should say influential) in proportion to the degree in which he is able to control his separate selves. In writing on Dean Inge Mr. Shaw himself, adopting much the same view, says: 'There are indeed two different persons in the case, a philosopher and a Dean; and one cannot but wonder what will happen if the two ever meet face to face. They need not; for experience shows us that though we are each at least half-a-dozen different persons, nothing is rarer than a meeting between any two of the six, much less a Parliament of the lot.'

Bernard Shaw consists of hundreds of persons. The Critic, the Poet, the Wit, the Dramatist, the Economist, the Actor, the Mob Orator, the Bishop, the Doctor, the General, etc., etc. My contention is that these different persons are always meeting and tripping one another up to the confusion of the reader. Though possibly an interesting essay could be written on The Battle of the Bernard Shaws, I shall only draw attention in the next section to the havoc which his Wit has caused.

II

It would be foolish to complain of Shaw's wit. It has given so much delight that it would be absurd to feel anything but gratitude for it. It has been Shaw's salvation again and again. In the early days it procured him a hearing; and having procured him a hearing saved him (if we can believe the testimony of his friends) from prison if not from assassination. It served as a sort of bodyguard. It allowed him to build a platform for himself and at the same time protected that platform from being burnt down by serious persons. It was necessary for him not to be taken too seriously at first. His sense of humour allowed him to turn and laugh at his misfortunes when they reached a certain point of hopelessness. No, I do not complain of his wit. I complain of the lack of control he exercised over his wit later on – or rather in the light of the above section, I complain of Shaw the Wit who instead of using his sugar-with-the-pill privilege, has foully abused it. Let us first glance at the harm it has done him in past politics.

It will not be denied that many times England has stood in sore need of the penetratingly sane advice which only Shaw has been capable of giving. At such times he has never refrained from giving his advice at considerable length. Unfortunately at such times he has also (and now for the sake of convenience and for fear of running the joke to death, I must revert again to the singular person) Shaw has never succeeded in keeping his wit severely in hand. If you know that it is an idiosyncrasy of the English people – especially of English Politicians – to consider a man who makes a jest in the middle of a serious exposition to be merely a jester, but if you nevertheless wish the English people to take your advice, the obvious thing to do is to omit the jests. Shaw has always been unable to do this. Though he will often sacrifice dramatic effect in order to point a doctrine he will always sacrifice both dramatic effect and doctrine in order to make a joke.

In his *How to Settle the Irish Question* he reviewed the situation in a no less penetrating way than he had formerly reviewed it in the Preface to *John Bull's Other Island* – a Preface that has received so much praise for its political accuracy. In this pamphlet, having placed the situation before the reader he says, 'I will now propound the solution'. The English reader gravely turns over the page and finds the heading 'Home Rule for England'. On a little reflection it becomes evident that this brilliant phrase sums up the whole situation – the dignity Ireland would attain with a Federal Government within the British Empire on the same terms that England is within the British Empire, and the tremendous gain England would get in at last having a chance to confine the activities of her Parliament to the English Questions in future instead of wasting hours of time discussing the Irish Question. But such a brilliant stroke as this doesn't pay in England: the reader throws down the pamphlet saying, 'Away with the trifler', and reads no more – or if he does read on, it is for pleasure and not for profit. It is therefore not surprising that when Shaw (knowing himself to be a good Committee man) did his best to get on the Irish Convention, Lloyd George found no difficulty in preventing his appointment.

Some critics are fond of comparing Shaw with Swift. There are too many differences to make it worth while. The greatest difference is this: that though both of them wrote their political pamphlets with intense sincerity, Shaw's pamphlets seldom produce any apparent effect, while those of Swift were able to change a policy of the Government and to save a nation from financial chaos. Swift's arrows went straight to their goal: Shaw's, weighted with wit, fall short. It is quite certain that Shaw could have shown-up Wood's Halfpence with greater brilliancy than Swift: it is quite certain that he would have failed to avert the disaster.

It is now agreed on all sides that the atmosphere in Europe in the years preceding the War was one of ridiculous secrecy, suspicion, and insecurity. No nation knew what other nations were going to do or what daggers, as it were, they had up their sleeves. The result naturally was that Alliances and Secret Treaties and Back-stairs policies were the order of the day. Every sane man knows that in such an atmosphere Fear is predominant. And every historian knows that Fear is at the bottom of all violence: in fact, the greater the fear the bloodier becomes the violence that follows, as in the case of the Committee of Public Safety in the French Revolution which was forced by fear to secure, not the life, but the death of everybody! Moreover, all negotiation between the Powers was carried on in that incredible jargon known as Diplomatic Style. Nothing is more maddening to the plain man (who does all the fighting) than to have the realities of Politics which he instinctively knows to be perfectly simple and straightforward, obscured by this monstrous mock courtesy which on the face of it is coarser than the vilest vulgarity.

Well, Bernard Shaw suggested in the *Daily Chronicle* eighteen months or so before the War that we should (absurd of course) say what we mean and mean what we say so that there could be no doubt what our policy was. He suggested that we should say clearly before Europe that if France was attacked by Germany we would defend France and if Germany was attacked by France or Russia we should defend Germany. I will not here go into a discussion on the merits of the suggestions, but I do not know how it will be proved that they were altogether idiotic. But no one took the slightest notice. His articles were taken as a joke. But it is useless for him to complain that this was because he was not 'a famous cricketer, jockey or glove fighter'. It was because he had incomplete control over his wit. It is ironic that his wit which makes so many people read him, still in the case of politics makes them think him unworthy of being seriously read. The means by which he won attention made him lose regard. His wit is like the Sword of old that rose and slew the slayer.

Thus when he wrote *The Truth about the War* in a much less humorous vein than anything else he has written, saying what everyone else was saying in two years' time and making many valuable suggestions, the effect of the pamphlet was purely bad because it was thought to be an unfeeling attack on England by an Irishman. Henceforth as Robert Lynd said, the War was considered to be between the Allies on one side and Germany, Austria, Turkey, and Bernard Shaw on the other, while Mr. H. Owen came forward with a pamphlet entitled *The Truth about the Shaw*, commenting on passages of Shaw's pamphlet in this sort of vein – 'Only a mind essentially filthy, only a person with some of the least desirable mental characteristics of the feminine gender, with the mind of a nagger and the voice of a shrew, could possibly pen a passage like that; and only Mr. Shaw having penned it could pass it for the printer.'

So also with *Peace Conference Hints*. It contains most of the remarks which other persons made after the Peace Conference had failed to do anything except make a Peace to end Peace and to prove that as certainly as wars produce peace treaties, peace treaties produce wars. Shaw's sane advice went unheeded for the same reason as all his other popular pamphlets have gone unheeded. While thousands of respectable people were insisting that seventeen suicides per day in some German towns was not enough, Shaw's emotional warning against 'the poisoning of the human soul by hatred, the darkening of the human mind by lies, and the hardening of the human heart by slaughter and destruction and starvation' carried no more weight with it than his appeal to the common-sense of the maxim 'treat your friend as one who may some day be your enemy and your enemy as one who may some day be your friend'. It is a tragic fact that Shaw, our most humane man, has always had less influence in suppressing inhumanity than any other public man.

In his plays his wit runs away with him even more frequently than in his pamphlets. Though bent upon forcing some doctrine on the attention of the reader or the audience he will not hesitate to obscure the doctrine for the sake of a laugh. In the last act of *Major Barbara* (the cardinal difficulties of which still embarrass critics as able as William Archer) he seems to do his utmost to prevent the audience or an impatient reader from following Undershaft's extremely difficult line of argument. After having made a large number of remarks the drift of which is not easy to catch, Undershaft shouts, 'Dare you make war on war?'

and as the audience begins to feel that now at last he is coming to the point, he goes on, 'My friend Lomax is sitting on the means'. Lomax, who is sitting on a recently manufactured high explosive shell, springs to his feet amidst roars of laughter from the audience. The point which they have been struggling to grasp (to which I will return later, concerning Undershaft's taste for death and destruction) is completely lost. Glorious comedy no doubt, and quite easily defended; but is it worth while confusing the vital argument like this? Is it fair?

In the Napoleonic scene in Part IV *Back to Methuselah*, he faces the question of what is to be done eventually with men whose genius lies only in the direction of commanding armies and conquering continents.

THE ORACLE. The way out of your difficulty is very simple.

NAPOLEON (*eagerly*). Good. What is it?

THE ORACLE. To die before the tide of glory turns.
Allow me. (*She shoots him*).

He is answered. Then suddenly before the audience has time to take in the answer and all that it implies, the Pentateuch sinks into low comedy and vulgar farce. Napoleon does not die but rises terrified to shriek curses at the departing Oracle and decorate her with such epithets as 'bitch! sow! wanton!' accompanied by a stage phrase to express his contempt at her being unable to hit a man at point-blank range. There can be little excuse for Mr. Shaw seizing the occasion to prove to us again that he cannot refrain from the opportunity of making a strong man lose his temper. He may have been at loss what to do with a corpse at this juncture if he had allowed Napoleon to die, but surely he could have died as easily and quite as reasonably as the Elderly Gentleman did.

I suppose some persons will call this Comic Relief and will say that Shaw has as much right to indulge in it as an Elizabethan. Perhaps he has: but what is the point of comic relief? I confess that its purpose in dramatic literature has always escaped me. It cannot be because light and shade are necessary in art or else we should have Tragic Relief in our comedies and farces. It can hardly be in order to relieve the tension of the audience, for the whole point of witnessing a play is to feel that tension as much as possible. It cannot even claim tradition, for Ibsen did not use it, Tolstoy did not use it, Brieux did not use it, when they considered that laughter would confuse the issue.

Whenever we are allowed to lose ourselves in some particularly fine passage we are always in danger of being rudely jerked to earth again by some paltry joke. After Caesar's great speech before the Sphinx, Cleopatra, who is hiding behind it, looks out and says 'Old Gentleman . . .' – and the audience is convulsed. Why these comic kicks? In what way are they superior to the man with the red nose, the gentleman with the hat, the nervous relation, the drunken friend, the silly old man, and all the other tricks which Mr. Shaw has done so much to expel from the boards? In *Back to Methuselah* they didn't even amuse anyone. In *Saint Joan* their presence is positively devilish. They ravage their way into the loftiest passages laying waste the exalted theme. In the epilogue for instance the cockney soldier chaffs Joan on imagining that she is the person to whom he held the cross upon the flaming pyre. 'They all imagine they are the only one, you know,' he says. This, if you please, in the middle of one of the finest passages in European Dramatic Literature!

It is time to look at Shaw's Wit in the proper perspective. It is time to recognise that it is ridiculously overrated, and that though it has done great service in its time it is really a part of him to endure rather than to admire. A proud gaiety conquering an otherwise too painful page is one thing: an uncontrollable little devil is quite another – a little devil that has again and again tarnished his art, concealed his poetry, mocked his influence, drowned his message, and will with absolute certainty pursue his memory beyond the grave.

III

Let us turn to the poet. It is hard for a witty man to be accepted as a teacher, but it is harder still for him to be accepted as a poet. In fact the wit and the politician have so successfully obscured the poet that not till *Back to Methuselah* was staged was it apparent to the critics that Mr. Shaw's prose was at times the finest in the language. People simply cannot believe that a man who is capable of addressing a crowd at a street corner is also capable of writing poetry. Mr. St. John Ervine is a good example as a victim of this delusion. Mr. Ervine — who is always much better when he is writing about nature than when he is writing about Shaw or the Theatre — informs us that Shaw has no sense of natural beauty and little feeling for architectural form. One wonders that he didn't add while he was about it, and no sense of Art! He hints that if Mr. Shaw during a country walk were to come across some druidical remains, instead of admiring the rude beauty of the ancient stones, he would be tempted to use them as a means of propaganda and chalk up 'Votes for Women!' The fact that this announcement was received by the Public and the Press as quite a sound remark to make about Bernard Shaw, gives one a clue to the sort of creature he is really supposed to be! Because Mr. Shaw is a wit and a propagandist it is forgotten that he bought Ayot St. Lawrence in Hertfordshire in order that he might escape as often as possible from the smoke of London, to commune with Nature; it is forgotten how insistently he has raged against the way in which our schools forbid any such holy communion for the child: it is forgotten with what lovely words he has shown how the poor are deprived by their poverty and townsmen cut off by the streets 'from the contemplation of the beauty of the earth, with its dresses of leaves, its scarves of cloud, and its contours of hill and valley'; it is forgotten how he has described through the mouth of Larry Doyle the feeling which is caused in Ireland by the air and the roads and the colours in the sky.

Of course I do not wish to suggest that he is a poet of Nature! Indeed my chief quarrel with him is that though he can write beautifully about the earth when he wishes, he is shy of doing so for some reason. I merely wish to point out that the same reason which makes people deny him a sense of natural beauty also makes them neglect the fact that his prose rises into great heights of poetry whenever he is writing in the language of mysticism, and sometimes when merely in the language of passion. Many worthy critics have denied Mr. Shaw this rank of poet. I am free to ask them how can they reconcile this opinion with the facts? How can they reconcile it with the heavenly music of Keegan's words which had an effect on me such as they must also have had upon thousands of others had these but the grace to acknowledge it? How can they reconcile it with the last words of Louis Dubedat as he uttered his creed and embraced his death? How can they reconcile it with the utterance of Major Barbara when she faced the evil but still saw the good, or with the words of Mrs. George when in a trance she delivered the abiding reproach of all women against men? How can they reconcile it with the mystic musing of Caesar as he stood in the desert a stranger amongst men symbolic of the everlasting loneliness of the Great? How can they reconcile it with the creation of Eugene Marchbanks, with the flaming prophecies of Captain Shotover, or the broken cries of Ellie Dunn? How can they reconcile it with the Epilogue to *Saint Joan*? Above all, how can they reconcile it with *Back to Methuselah*?

A brief glance at *Back to Methuselah* will help us with this question. Just a glance may be the more welcome since the reception given to this masterpiece on its performance in London was a national scandal. Though it is one play with five separate parts linked together with the careful junction of a watch chain the critics judged each part separately as if it had been *Charlie's Aunt*. There can be no doubt whatever that this drama is Mr. Shaw's masterpiece. It is far greater than *Man and Superman* or *Saint Joan*. The Dream in *Man and Superman* is magnificent of course, but it is too clever, too showy: you are inclined to admire the author more than his theme. The rest of the play is the mere frame of the Dream and is inclined to leave a bad taste in the mind's mouth, if I may so express myself, owing to the over-brilliancy of Tanner, the over-silliness of Octavius, and the over-ugliness of Anne. *Saint Joan* — great as it is — can no more be ranked with *Back to Methuselah* than *Julius Caesar* can be ranked with *Hamlet*. *Back to Methuselah* is a drama of colossal strength: it is built upon all Shaw's learning and thought. It does what it sets out to do — gives a credible vision of what we were, what we are, and what we may be. If Part V is approached slowly and sympathetically by the reader (it is much better to read it than to see it) he will find himself gradually overcome by a feeling of spiritual emotion and elevation such as perhaps he has never known before. He will be tripped up by no cleverness or brilliancy but will rise above all earthly things into those regions which mighty poetry alone can create.

So anxious am I that the reader will at least consider the greatness of Part V, that I will venture to escort him to it by refreshing his memory with a brief summary of the cycle. The cycle suggests the way that evolution may take in saving us from our economic problems. In Part I we find Adam and Eve dwelling together in the Garden of Eden, with the prospect of living for ever unless an accident makes an end of them. But they can bear neither the thought of sudden complete extinction, nor the idea of living for ever, so they gladly listen to the suggestion made to them by a friendly serpent, of using a means called Birth, by which the race will be perpetuated, while Death will lose its sting but gain its victory. Unfortunately Birth brings forth Cain, who invents early death by killing, till living becomes so precarious that the average length of life instead of being about a thousand years (as in Adam's case) begins to be about three score and ten. Eve however still has hopes that her clever sons, her thinkers, her dreamers, her poets, may yet trample over the Cain-ites. In the next part (the present day) two philosophic biologists come forward with the suggestion that in view of the fact that we have proved ourselves incapable of managing our complicated affairs with such a short individual life, we should will to live longer (say 300 years). They hold that biology points to the fact that, whatever a man wills sufficiently, be it a longer nose or a longer life, shall at last be added unto him. They place their suggestions before two politicians who turn it down because it has not sufficient election interest.

It should be observed here that Mr. Shaw has satirised living politicians, just as Swift did in *Gulliver's Travels*, as Dryden did in his political fables, and as, indeed, all satirists are bound to do in the nature of things.

In Part III (A.D. 2170) we are introduced to the first two persons who have succeeded in living longer. The purpose of this part is perhaps to demonstrate the biological theory that after a certain amount of willing (as in learning to ride a bicycle) the change is likely to come suddenly and secretly, like a thief in the night. These two long-livers being fortunately man and woman, decide to people the earth with descendants and so depart to accomplish this consummation. In Part IV (A.D. 3000) we find that one whole country is exclusively inhabited by long-livers, whose advice is often sought by short-lived (or normal lived) visitors. In this piece there is much satire against the Neo-Darwinians, together with a certain amount of not altogether happy farce, introduced perhaps in order that the majesty of the last Part, which carries us forward to As Far As Thought Can Reach, may be the more impressive.

There we find man and woman born from eggs, at the age of seventeen (to illustrate the theory of Condensed Recapitulation), to enjoy for four years, the luxury of art, love, and laughter, after which they gradually cease to care for any of these things, and become Ancients, whose understanding of Reality is so absorbing as to make them oblivious to all comfort and insensitive to all beauty. They have put away the Old Adam in them, and embrace the burden of eternal life. They still fear a fatal accident even as Adam was afraid, but they know that just as they have conquered the need to sleep, conquered the need to eat, conquered the desires and the pains of the flesh, so will they eventually be able to get rid of their bodies altogether, and be free to wander as pure Intelligences across the planets as the wind that bloweth where it listeth.

Thus, the author suggests, may the economic slavery of our lives be overcome. If we help evolution along this path, then the time will come when neither the voice of the economist who demonstrates our political chaos, nor the voice of the geologist who predicts the coming of the next ice-age and the eventual passing of the earth, need trouble us, for we will have overcome the world, and will exist only as souls with the sure and certain hope of everlasting life.

In the final Part when the Ancients have expressed their philosophy they disappear from the scene. It darkens. Then with tremendous dramatic effect (enjoyed ever so much more by the reader than the hearer who at the supreme moment may find himself at the mercy of elocutionists) the characters who were present in the first scene now come forward again. Once more we see Cain who came into the world before the first murder, Adam and Eve who brought forth Cain, the Serpent who came before Adam and before Eve and taught them how to bring forth Cain, and lastly Lilith who came before the Serpent, and in whom the father and mother were one. Each in turn delivers his or her judgment upon Life as they behold it now, and then vanish again into the darkness. At last Lilith alone is left to prophesy. We hold our breath to hear her judgment. Her words are sublime. They are unworldly: but we of the earth are raised to an understanding of them. They are unemotional but they fill us with passionate desire to labour for righteousness. They are in a sense the final utterance of Bernard Shaw after over sixty years of activity and meditation. And I must be allowed to free myself for a moment from the blinding dust of literary criticism and to assert with confidence that it is the highest point yet reached in English poetry, nor is there any passage in Shakespeare which comes up to it in majesty. It has reached that point where 'style' is of no account, but where mathematics, philosophy, religion, science, and poetry have met together and become as one. A vision of all life is spread before us and we see clearly from whence we have come and whither we may go; and as the fiery thought mounts upward into the high and lonely regions of the imagination, so, in proportion, is the ascension of the 'prose style'.

A closing scene like the above is peculiarly suited to Bernard Shaw's genius. He is well aware of this himself and has repeated it almost exactly in the Epilogue to *Saint Joan*, where the ghosts of the characters in the play pass judgment upon the burning of the Maid. It will be seen therefore that there can be no sort of sense in comparing a good play like *Saint Joan* with a masterpiece like *Back to Methuselah*. The one tells a story of a life: the other tells the story of Life itself. In the Epilogue to *Saint Joan* we see the triumph of the

Maid and the failure of the Saints: in the Epilogue to *Back to Methuselah* we are shown the triumphant ascension of Life. It is insulting the author to think of comparing the merits of the first with the merits of the second. But I daresay just as there were some people who wish away the Epilogue to *Saint Joan* simply because it is an Epilogue, so no doubt there are plenty who, now that I have pointed it out, will wish away the Epilogue to *Back to Methuselah*.

In case this book of mine should ever in some future age be lifted from the dusty corner of some great library by the curious antiquary, I will note in passing for his delectation, that on the performance of this Dramatic Cycle, there arose in the columns of the premier newspaper a controversy between the Great Critic and the Author, so violent as to verge on the shedding of blood, concerning the question as to whether the i in 'isolate' should be pronounced long or short. There was no other controversy.

Now let us return to the main point with which I am dealing in this section — Shaw the poet. I know well that the word poet is desperately vague — it is like the word Love, the word Nature, the word God, it can mean almost anything. I use it here simply in the sense of a man who employs a medium of expression which carries the reader a step higher than ordinary prose can carry him, though the words are not technical. (Swearing is the opposite to poetry, for it carries the reader a step lower than ordinary prose can carry him, though the words need not be technical.) I hope the day has long since gone by when what is written in verse is looked upon as poetry and what is within the covers of a book is looked upon as literature. You can no more draw a line between prose and poetry than you can between journalism and literature. Some prose is often much better poetry than some verse, just as some journalism is often much better literature than some books. We are fond of separating things up and cutting things in half that should remain whole. It is a foolish weakness and it is wrecking the world. Europe is cut up into bits but she really is all one piece. When we understand that the whole world is a Unity, then the paradox will lose its sting and the epigram forget its cunning; there will be nothing startling in the fact that in Politics the most important item in Domestic Affairs is Foreign Affairs, and that in Literature good poetry is sometimes written in prose while bad prose is often written in verse.

In a number of plays such as *John Bull's Other Island*, *Major Barbara*, *Getting Married*, *Back to Methuselah*, Bernard Shaw ends on a note of mysticism. Shaw's prefaces, contrary to the popular fallacy about them, lead up to but do not go as far as and seldom do much to explain the plays. And the end of many of his plays go further still as it were. Now the words of Keegan, Major Barbara in her closing speech, Caesar before the

Sphinx, Mrs. George in her trance and Lilith, all have a certain quality in common. It is the quality of Mysticism. To express his mysticism the author must either employ technical terms like Kant or poetic terms. Shaw has chosen the latter. All the arts are more or less a unity and when they reach a certain pitch of intensity they seem to become the same thing. It is when Shaw the philosopher, the mystic, the scientist, the mathematician is speaking that we get the poet also. No one I think will deny this quality when he recalls how deeply moving are the words in the above-mentioned passages when so many different characters in so many different ways look into the streets of Heaven.

But it is not only at his moments of mysticism that Shaw becomes a poet. There are speeches of Louis Dubedat, Captain Shotover, Ellie Dunn, speeches at the end of Saint Joan, and in the beginning of *Back to Methuselah*, which though they do not strike the note of mysticism mentioned above do not strike merely the note of eloquence and rhetoric — think of the eloquence of Larry Doyle and the poetry of Keegan — scattered so profusely throughout the plays, especially in *Man and Superman*. What I am driving at may be clearer if I remind the reader of H. G. Wells' *Men Like Gods*. It is perhaps Wells' finest book. It seems to me to reach at moments great heights of eloquence and passion and yearning. The reader is swept off his feet with enthusiasm and with hope. But at no point whatever does it cease to be eloquence and become poetry. Thus if we compare the passionate words of Wells with the enormous number of passages in Shaw which are passionless in an earthly sense but are perhaps more moving, my distinction may be plain.

However that may be, it is in his passages of mysticism that Shaw ascends with absolute certainty the Parnassian Mount and writes in a slow and stately rhythm passages that will remain, long after his ideas have become stale, to 'perpetuate and repeat his name'.

IV

In Mr. Henderson's biography of Shaw there are many interesting photographs of him. But there is one that especially appeals to the imagination. He is addressing a crowd of dockers on behalf of Alderman Saunders at Portsmouth. An open air meeting on a winter's day. A long ugly wall on one side closes in the crowd and two lifeless, leafless trees give an air of sad coldness to the background. On the platform above the crowd of darkly dressed dockers stands Bernard Shaw, his head thrust forward, his expression hard and threatening, his right fist clenched. No signs of Shaw the poet and mystic here! Still less signs of Shaw the author, the man of letters. One inevitably thinks of those other scenes where other great men of letters in the past have spent their spare time. One thinks of the Mermaid Tavern where Shakespeare, Ben Jonson and Fletcher exchanged pleasantries and where Marlowe died drunk; of the Coffee House where Addison sat attentive to his own applause; of the Cheshire Cheese where Samuel Johnson spent about sixty years of marvellous talk — only one year of it being reported by Boswell; of the smiling hearth of the Authors' Club where generation after generation of writers have sat discussing how Barrabas is a Publisher; of the polite drawing-room where celebrated hostesses 'bring together' famous men; and of many other scenes far removed from the dark surroundings of the docker's home. Bernard Shaw does not care for these things. 'I care only,' he said, 'for my mission as I call it, and my work.' He is an economist and cannot bear waste of time or rest — for like the famous Frenchman he knows that he has 'all eternity to rest in'! He has a great love for Art but not for Artists. He dislikes and fears his fellow men: he has no tombstone-love for them at all. That accounts for the fact that he so intensely desires their advancement or, failing that, their extinction. He would use all the resources of Art to help us forward but will not countenance Art for its own sake while we remain as we are. 'Chastity without Charity lies chained in Hell!' cried Piers the Plowman. 'Faith without works is useless,' urges every Evangelist. 'Art for Art's sake is not enough,' has been Bernard Shaw's simple motto and practice ever since he left Dublin in 1876.

Bernard Shaw has been praised a great deal, and has praised himself for facing facts. But what has always appeared to me to be the chief point about Shaw's prefaces, pamphlets, essays, and speeches is not so much his facing facts as *knowing* facts. The necessity for the social reformer to gather up all the available and telling facts about a subject before he attempts to convert anybody is quite possibly one of the most important lessons Shaw has to teach to politicians and social reformers. He realised this at a very early age as is proved by his remark in *Cashel Byron's Profession* concerning Lucian who had gone to Lydia to persuade her what an illegal and brutal thing prize fighting is – 'his secretarial duties had taught him to provide himself with a few well-arranged relevant facts before attempting to influence the opinions of others upon any subject'.

That is what is meant by saying that knowledge is power. But, I may say in passing, it would be an abuse of that fine phrase to suppose that knowledge is power to everyone. There are plenty of men walking up and down Oxford at this moment whose power of assimilating and remembering facts is tremendous, but whose power of using them leaves much to be desired. Knowledge is their weakness rather than their strength. Their backs are bent, their gait infirm under the heavy burden which they bear. New facts can no longer stir them — for the fuel has put out the fire.

It is agreed that for lack of dulness a Shaw preface or pamphlet is unique in the history of literature. The reason is that Shaw has been able to add to his four great gifts, active imagination, humane heart, clear mind, and literary skill (all in the superlative), the power and the will to get hold of the facts upon every subject with which he has to deal. During his first twenty years in London he positively swam in facts. Everyone knows that he had nine years' struggle when he came to London but few realise precisely what his programme during his first twenty years before he fell ill and nearly died consisted of. It works itself out to nine years of desperately shabby privation of everything except, fortunately, food and weatherproof shelter, during which he wrote five novels, made six pounds, read daily in the British Museum, and became a leader of the Fabians; then he did four years as Art critic, and literary reviewer, partly overlapped by six as Music critic, followed by four as Dramatic Critic, while all the time he dashed about with incredible activity lecturing on Socialism twice a week with no holidays and wrestling with facts facts facts! When it is realised what this frantic activity means (for instance, how much literature he grappled with in the British Museum and how many Committee Meetings he sat on in the Fabian Society, or how much work was required by a novice to master abstract Political Economy as Jevons had left it), it ceases to be surprising that all his books written afterwards stand as unshakable upon a foundation of fact as an impregnable fortress upon a foundation of rock.

Thus it at once becomes plain why he tilts against vivisection and prisons in practically every play and preface. He knows the facts.

This factual knowledge accounts for his unparalleled success during question-time at public meetings – for a display of facts always overcomes an audience during question-time in the same proportion as it bores them during lecture-time. Shaw has himself 'pooh-poohed' the idea that he is particularly good at questions and insisted that his answers are good only because he is always asked the same questions. This may be so, but nevertheless there is something absolutely phenomenal in his power in this direction. A man gets up and asks a question which seems a real stumper: but Shaw without a second's hesitation springs to his feet and answers it – or eludes it – with a flash. There is something almost sinister in such deadly assurance. He can either answer the question by an illuminating epigram which lights up the whole problem, such as his answer to 'do you believe in the Immaculate Conception.' 'Of course I do: all conceptions are immaculate:' or he can elude it with a reply such as that given to a lady who asked, 'if you met a man in the street without a coat would you give him yours?' 'But there would, in that case, still be one of us without a coat.' But his power lies in having facts to hurl at anyone at a moment's notice. I always remember in this connection a question which was asked of him after he had been explaining his favourite theory of making everyone work for not less than two hours a day – 'how would the engine-driver of an express train from Euston to Scotland manage to do two hours only?' (Laughter.) 'I see no difficulty,' he replied; 'he would be relieved by another engine-driver waiting for his turn;' he then went on to make some further remarks about engines and engine-drivers, displaying a very considerable knowledge of that branch of work – probably much more than his questioner.

As regards his actual speaking, Ben Jonson's comment upon Bacon as a speaker is equally justified if applied to Shaw – 'it is the fear of every man lest he should make an end'. In view of the fact that he is not a born speaker and does not enjoy it much, it may be interesting to consider what are his tricks. His tricks are that he has no tricks but one theory instead, namely – never give information in a speech. Once at a lecture given by an American I noticed Shaw sitting in the corner with his eyes closed. Afterwards I heard someone reproach him for having gone to sleep. 'I defy anyone,' he answered, 'to remember a single thing the lecturer said. It was all information. You should never give information in a lecture: only ideas. Information can be got in a text-book on the subject.'

His power of holding the attention of an audience springs from his use of the above theory, his personality, his articulation, and his general platform manner: otherwise he is disappointing as a speaker. As to his personality I need say little in a book of this nature; the tall figure, the thin back, the weak-looking legs, the now slightly shaking hands, the superb head, need no further comment. In the evening when he always dresses in black he looks like a sea-captain or his own Captain Shotover. He seems hundreds of years old in that dress, while if you see him dash down the Strand in the afternoon in his light green cape, he seems still quite young. As to his articulation, I fancy it is the most perfect articulation possible – at least it is frankly impossible to imagine anything better. He delivers it with an Irish intonation (for all Irishmen who are much away from their own country adopt an Irish accent in England and an English accent in Ireland). As to his general movements on the platform, it will be sufficient to say that he has conquered the arms and hands problem. He knows what to do with them when not making a gesture. 'How?' Apparently by the simple method of wearing his clothes in such a way that he can fold his arms with comfort – and not feel that he is striking an attitude.

Though his plays reveal a great command of oratory and lift us at times to the highest flights of rhetoric, and though he loves the dramatic moment, he never plays the orator, never uses rhetoric, and never is theatrical. Some people say that the age of oratory is over and that it no longer makes its old appeal. They are wrong. It is only necessary to hear Dr. Annie Besant speak to have all one's theories concerning the declension of the purple patch, the expulsion of the period, and the modern powerlessness of the peroration, shattered for ever by that magnificent and accomplished lady. But Shaw never makes an emotional appeal, never speaks with 'felicity', or subtlety or decoration, never carefully bursts into a fiery passage, seldom indulges in a digression or an epigram, while nearly all his jokes arise out of personal idiosyncrasy. He simply says what he has to say with extreme simplicity and then sits down. When he rises to his feet he never refers to anything the chairman has just said, never says what a pleasure it is to address so distinguished an audience, and never apologises for his presumption in addressing them at all on such a subject. That was Ruskin's way of starting a lecture, immediately after which he would attack his audience as if they had personally insulted him and pour forth a torrent of vituperation unequalled in the history of Lecturing. Shaw putting on one side both vituperation and emotional appeal, concentrates his whole mind on simple intellectual statement. The result is that though he is sometimes a little disappointing, a speech of his can at times make oratory and vituperation appear peculiarly small. It is like listening to Common

Sense speaking, for Shaw has that delightful gift of seeing the obvious and not concluding at once from its obviousness that it is of no account. He does not, as he says, pull our legs but simply pulls crooked legs straight: he does not say black is white and white is black but says simply that white is white and black is black. Common Sense and the power to see an obvious thing are irresistible attractions because we all feel that our own thoughts are being expressed – which is the highest compliment possible to pay to an artist.

It is interesting to add that when he rises or sits down there is comparatively little applause as a rule. For people come to listen to him not to applaud him: when he sits down they are too sorry to thank him. For most speakers the applause at the end is polite applause – if not an emotional thanksgiving for the end.

CHAPTER EIGHT

The Soul of Drama: The Destiny of Characterisation:
Technique: Undershaft's Profession: The Meaning of
Heartbreak House

✽

I

In literary technique whatsoever is new, whatsoever is strange, whatsoever is unusual, whatsoever is untried, whatsoever is unknown to the prevailing fashion, is always assailed by the critics of the time with curious bitterness and rancour, as impracticable, vain, absurd, shocking and altogether impossible. The reason for this is that a man who introduces a new technique also introduces new views: and it is the views that are really objected to. That accounts for the fact that even Ibsen, whose technique though novel was extraordinarily good from the story-telling point of view, was attacked as a bungler and inefficient fool. For our desire to feel that those with whom we disagree are fools and bunglers is so strong as to over-ride all other considerations.

Bernard Shaw's technique was new in the same proportion as his ideas were new – and since his ideas were abundant and unpalatable to the prevailing taste the attack upon his technique was unprecedented in violence. It took the form (and it still takes the form) of saying that he has no technique and that his plays are not plays. Such people argue upon this subject on such a plane of unreality that they never dream of taking into account two flagrant facts that stare them in the face. First, the fact that *Getting Married* has been more often played and is in greater demand than any other play of his. Now *Getting Married* is a flagrant example of everything, which according to these critics, a play should not be. It is all talk. It has no material action, no movement, no dramatic scenes, no good curtains. It has nothing that a play should have – and yet it is the most often acted of all these plays that are not plays! Second, if he is not a playwright it is odd that he should be played with such enthusiasm from end to end of the Continent where he is (unfortunately) a classic – six plays of his being performed in one week in Berlin at a time when Germany seemed on her last legs.

But the popularity of *Getting Married* need not surprise anyone who realises the chief necessity of a play. Every day a larger number of people is beginning to recognise that *dialogue is the soul of drama*. That is perhaps the only fact we know quite definitely upon the subject – drama is dialogue, dialogue is drama, that is all we know about it and all we need to know. Conflict there must be, passion there must be, strife there must be, but the conflict and the passion and the strife need not spring from material movements – nay, must not always do so, if a play is to be something better than the cinema. No amount of movement, blood and thunder can make up for bad dialogue, but brilliant dialogue can be sufficient. Bernard Shaw has always held fast to these facts. He knows that the phrase that smashes and the jest that kills excite an audience more than the clash of material swords upon the stage — for there is more reality in the one kind of battle than in the other. He knows that material conflict is often interesting but that intellectual conflict is always inspiring. Thus every Shaw play is an army which gives battle.

Let us look a little closer at this point. The greater number of people who make up an audience do not ask themselves what they have gone to the theatre for: few would dream of saying that they go there simply to be amused as is alleged by theatrical theorists. Even the most unsophisticated person knows that to be interested is better than to be amused. And once they are inside the theatre they enjoy good dialogue before anything else. If they do not want dialogue they can go to the cinema where they can get as much action and thrill as is good for them. Even the criticism of those to whom drama is 'the play' and dialogue 'repartee' confirms me in the belief that dialogue is the soul of drama. I have heard these people complain that *The Prisoner of Zenda* was disappointing because 'the repartee was so bad', while they liked William Archer's *Green Goddess* not because it had efficient technique and a plot but because 'the things the Rajah said were so priceless'. Again I have noticed that the scene that is appreciated most in *John Bull's Other Island* is the talk in front of the cottage in Act III — though it is a pure public discussion and 'gets no one any farther'.

Why is this? The answer to this sort of question is as simple as the answer to Why do we have War? We have war because we like fighting – (a fact which is full of hope, for when we one day grow out of this taste – as we will do no less certainly than adolescents grow out of the taste for playing at toy soldiers – we will have no more wars). The reason why dialogue is so important in drama is because conversation is the bread and wine of life. We attach an astonishing importance to conversation. We cannot get on without it. If silence is imposed upon us for long we risk death or madness. We dare not sit in a room with an acquaintance without indulging in it – and yet most of us are miserably poor talkers. The result is that anyone who is a good talker is in tremendous demand. It does not matter what he is like: let him be hard, unfriendly, ungenerous and a victim of the Seven Deadly Sins, yet all shall be forgiven him if only he is a good talker. On the other hand, let a person be as respectable as you please, a walking example of the Seven Deadly Virtues, but a boring talker – and he will be avoided by his kind. I need not labour this point. We all know it to be true. We all have known and envied the popular boy or girl at school and college who was popular for that reason alone. We know how Fanny Burney said it was worth walking forty miles to hear the conversation of

Samuel Johnson. We know that in our hearts we like our friends in proportion to the degree in which they bore or interest us by their conversation.

Again, people love to hear a good speech almost more than anything else. The cry of 'speech, speech' on a first night or at a wedding breakfast, is a genuine expression of the human desire to hear an address on any possible occasion. It is true that if the speaker is dull they suffer torture, but there is always the possibility that he may be good. There are few things that people enjoy more than a good rowdy public meeting. There is nothing boring about a successful mob oration: there is real bursting life all round. The result is that the most popular scene in Shakespeare is the forum oration in *Julius Caesar*, the most popular acting play of Ibsen is *The Enemy of the People* in which Dr. Stockmann proclaims that the majority is always wrong. And the terrible trial scene in *Justice* petrifies the audience with horror and gloom.

Now Bernard Shaw flatters our love of conversation by giving us whole plays like *Getting Married* in which the conflict of tongues, the strife of thought against thought is interrupted by no plot or side-issue – and its popularity justifies its singleness of appeal, no less than its implied protest that if Congreve is accepted as a great dramatist in spite of his appalling plots (if chaos can be dignified by that name) and if Oscar Wilde can fascinate by the epigram alone, then a play full of wit and wisdom with no plot to trip over or call old-fashioned, is well worth writing. And I submit that we have never had a dramatist before who possessed such exact knowledge of what will come cleanly off the lips of an actor as Mr. Shaw. The chief attraction of his plays lies in the fact – I am quite prepared to face it – that most of his characters speak as if they were addressing a public meeting. He learnt what can and what cannot leave the tongue in his early days of continual tub-thumping – a splendid training for a dramatist. The athletic purity of the speech of his characters (as a special example I recommend the Inca of Perusalem's outburst to the Lady near the end of the play under that name) is overwhelming.

Perhaps the reader, at this point, may feel inclined to ask me whether I consider the manager or the critic who says 'mind you don't have any talky-talky in your play' a fool and a liar. Unhesitatingly I do. Of course I know quite well that any playwright who adopts absolutely Shaw's methods must also have Shaw's brains, but nevertheless dialogue is the most important thing in any play. But how long are we going to tolerate this no-talky-talky gentleman? He is the enemy of us all. He would cut from Shakespeare all the speeches and leave nothing but the stolen plots behind. He would rob us of the best drama in the world. It is time that in the name of Shakespeare, Sheridan and Shaw, we proclaimed a crusade against him and his fellows as we should against all robbers and liars and desecrators of holy things.

II

More nonsense has been talked about Bernard Shaw's characterisation than about any other portion of his work. The remark 'Oh, Bernard Shaw doesn't stage human beings at all; they are mere talking machines, mere puppets set up to spout Shaw' is repeated with a persistency and a petulance which justifies me taking up the challenge. But let us first get some perspective on the subject. So far (1924) he has written thirty-seven plays: as a rule in each play there are not less than ten characters: therefore if we are going to generalise it is as well to realise that we are generalising about three to four hundred characters.

Now I think a case could be made out against at least one character in every play as being a 'spouter' of Shaw rather than anything else, though no case can ever be made out against any single character in all the plays being non-human. They always retain their humanity no matter how much they preach. And later on I will admit that Mr. Shaw has little power of convincing us that any of his historical figures even remotely resemble the originals, though again they are splendidly alive. But as regards the greater number of his characters I am convinced that the general shout of derision against them is caused not because they are unreal but because they are too real, just as the shout of derision that first greeted Turner's pictures was not because they were untrue to Nature but because they were too true. We blanch before the blazing truth. When we read a book or go into the theatre we still are not prepared to renounce all romantic feelings: we still like to think in terms of good and bad of hero and villain. But in Shaw's plays we find no heroes and no villains — for all men are heroes and all men are villains. In Shaw's plays we find no pure comic or pure tragic characters — for all men are comic and all men are tragic. His lovers are not always loving, his old are not always stupid, and his young are not always charming. They are not rational stage characters guaranteed to do the right thing at the right moment. They are human, and their souls are laid bare with almost horrible penetration. We cannot bear it: we insist that the author is joking. 'I am,' he replies. 'My way of joking is by telling the truth. It is the funniest joke in the world.'

How far is this bold claim justified? I venture to say that wherever the truth lies in this matter, it is far nearer the above claim than it is near the 'puppets' claim which enables certain smart writers to show off their epigrams no less than it allows stupid people to demonstrate their stupidity. When one turns to a play like *The Doctor's Dilemma* to be faced with 'B.B.' and the other doctors and Dubedat and the Cornish girl and to find a whole act given up almost entirely to the exhibition of character (and such character!) one asks oneself in amazement what is meant by those who state that the author merely puts up puppets to preach with. When we are told that Shaw cannot and does not portray the working man, and then read *Major Barbara* we are forced to question our sanity. For here is an intensive study in the psychology of the poor man. Within the boundaries of one Act we are shown the influence of poverty upon the poor, the cynical attitude of the poor towards philanthropy tempered with religion, their lack of sympathy with one another, their admiration for the rich, their snobbery – points which the social reformer too often forgets. Again it is impossible to praise the characterisation of *John Bull's Other Island* too highly. Every character is drawn to life with the exception of Father Keegan whom few of us are lucky enough to have met. Nora Reilly and Mat Haffigan (to mention only two) are not any easier to forget than Broadbent who now hangs in that national gallery of pen-portraits ranging from Sir Giles Overreach to Sherlock Holmes. I cannot go through each play separately: I can only call attention to the procession of character that passes through *Misalliance* and *Getting Married*, and remind the reader how the fundamental traits of human nature were so well shown in *Arms and the Man* that the Bulgarians were amazed at its veracity, and how in that extremely 'preachy' play of *Blanco Posnet* the character of Blanco is so carefully drawn that the sophisticated person is not so impressed as the unsophisticated. It is hard to avoid the conclusion that Shaw's strongest talent (when he chooses to exert it) lies in the portrayal of human beings as they are, and that his fame will ultimately rest neither upon his ideas nor wit but upon his poetry and characterisation. Our difficulty in realising this at first sight may be because we are so used to stagey characters that real ones seem unreal just as a play without some further variation of the eternal triangle seems quite wrong. Moreover, Shaw's characters are exceptionally articulate, they express their several points of view more clearly than in actual life. But this is not a legitimate ground of complaint against the artist — for after all the word art is (in a sense) only short for articulation. It is true that their reality does not slap you in the face, as it were, like the characters of John Galsworthy's plays. For Shaw lends all his characters his own brilliancy; but I do not know how it will be proved that this quality hides the real bones of his characters any more than the poetry in Shakespeare or the caricature in Dickens hides the intensely real bones of their creations.

Intense realism is the chief characteristic of most of his plays — a realism carried so far that he will sometimes, as in the case of *The Doctor's Dilemma*, deliberately refrain from the perfect artistic end-ing and offer reality instead. He knew that in real life the story would not end with the death of Dubedat and that secrets don't keep themselves. So — greatly to the scandal of the critics — he added an extra scene in which a real piece of life and real character were portrayed. This scene affects every one in a different way I suppose. I remember reading the play for the first time in order to conquer a certain Christmas evening. I felt sleepy while reading Act IV but the electric effect of the last Act completely woke me up.

Before going on to notice Shaw's women, historical characters, and unreal characters it is interesting to note Shaw's own reflections upon his creations. He is fond of telling us how he has pillaged various characters from this or that source — though it is difficult to detect the smallest resemblance between the supposed original and copy. He tells us how some characters like Lady Britomart are drawn straight from life. I confess whenever I see an impossible person like Lina Szczepanowska come on the stage I have a strong suspicion that she must have been taken from real life. He tells us that he lifts characters bodily from the pages of Dickens. If this is so why does he tell us that Dubedat is compounded from several living originals? I suggest that Dickens has had an important hand in his creation. Surely the likeness between Harold Skimpole in *Bleak*

House and Dubedat, especially in his way of 'not knowing anything about money', is too near to be a mere coincidence. It will be remembered that Dickens took Leigh Hunt as the original of Skimpole. Thus if Shaw took Skimpole as the original of Dubedat, Leigh Hunt whatever he may or may not have done, at least has to his credit the gift of a Skimpole and a Dubedat to the world.[1]

But Shaw is more interested in women than in men. How do they stand the test of realism? On the whole they will bear as much scrutiny as his men. Somehow or other everyone (including myself) thinks of Shaw's women as hard and bad-tempered and forward and cruel. But we never pause to consider that the impression merely arises from the fact that creatures like Aspasia, Gloria, Vivie Warren, Anne Whitefield, and Blanche are those whom we chiefly remember. Shaw probably does not like them any more than we do, though he no doubt thinks he ought to like them, just as he thinks he ought to like young

---

[1] "This is not a happy shot. Skimpole pretends to be a child: he is a sponge and a failure. Dubedat is virile, predatory, professionally splendidly efficient, with an heroic faith in art, a blackguard only on a plane where he is a foreigner. Dickens made a mess of Skimpole, who is not an artist at all, nor even intended to be one, but a Bohemian cadger. The truth is, Dickens made a portrait of Leigh Hunt, and, finding that his friends recognised it, defaced it until it no longer resembled a human being.' G. B. S.

men though he cannot bear them. It will be remembered how at the close of the last century George Eliot's Dinah Morris and Dickens' Agnes were good examples of the type of heroine then produced. Shaw (the slave of reactions, not the cause of them; the slave of a Movement and not the creator of it) is so terrified lest he should produce a Dinah Morris or an Agnes that he goes to the opposite extreme. I have a suspicion that he does this also as a gesture against the drawing-room young ladies towards whom he has always shown in his novels and many corners of his work a kindly contempt. He has often insisted on their unnaturalness, their appalling manners, their pseudo-refinement, their pseudo-good taste, their pseudo-charm, their ignorance and emptiness. I have a strong suspicion that in order to try and knock some sense into these unpresentable girls Shaw has left them out of his plays altogether and deliberately drawn the unsentimental business-like type of girl instead.

Fortunately however he does not give us many of these girls. Barbara, Lady Waynflete, Nora Reilly, The Flower Girl, Ellie Dunn, Jennifer Dubedat, Candida and others demonstrate Shaw's penetration into the minds of many different types of women – a penetration which is simply the result (as he said recently with obvious truth) of going on the assumption that women act and think precisely as he himself acts and thinks. Candida deserves a word to herself. Never has our unreal way of judging whether Shaw's characterisation is true or not been better demonstrated than by the criticisms which were made about Candida — and are still made. She is looked upon as a charming woman — as one of Shaw's few charming women. Yet she actually is, as her creator meant her to be, a peculiarly hateful sort of woman. She philanders in the most brutal way possible, allowing the poet to fall in love with her without having any intention of letting him go a step farther than is convenient for her while at the same time allowing her husband to suffer just as much as Marchbanks suffers. She is an entirely selfish trifler. When finally she paints a picture of deadly efficient household bliss the poet suddenly realises that life is something bigger than that and with that secret in his heart rushes out into the night.

The woman, however, about whom most controversy rages and in whom Shaw is himself most interested, is Anne Whitefield. He knows quite well and has admitted that she is not necessarily a typical woman — there being lots of almost anti-sex women about. His general philosophic view of women is, however, that when a woman falls in love she pursues her chosen one with all her might and that the Life Force compels her to do so. It is well known that both Dickens and Shakespeare also took this view without mentioning any Life Force attached to it. This subject is entirely a question of opinion and experience.

But I will venture to offer one suggestion here without dragging in the Life Force at all. Would it not be strange if women did not pursue men slightly more than men pursue women for the purpose of getting married? A woman is not only the daughter of her mother: she is the daughter of fifty thousand generations of human life. She has always been, and is still in nine cases out of ten, in the appalling position of being the economic slave of man. If she does not marry there is no place for her as a respected citizen even if she has enough money to save her from privation. In self-protection marriage is essential to her even if we overlook the natural desire to have children. A man does not gain by marriage one-tenth of what a woman gains. Why then should he be the pursuer rather than the pursued? It is inevitable that she must pursue even if her manner of pursuing is by running away. She does not come into the world unarmed. She has all the weapons that have been handed down to her from generation to generation of husband-winning. She does not know that she has these weapons: she will passionately deny to herself and to all the world that she 'does anything on purpose'. It is all done for her just as the breathing of her lungs is done without conscious effort. Often to her amazement the right word or the right tear falls at the right moment from her lips or eyes. Her weapons are unconscious — and therefore devilishly powerful. She is the receiver of a rich legacy of generations of practise.

Owing to the fact that Shaw can so accurately portray life as he sees it with his eyes, he is not so successful in dealing with persons whom he can only imagine. That accounts for the fact that his historical figures are so unconvincing. They live of course: Shaw can make anything live – even the Law of Rent and the Theory of Value. But it is not possible to believe that you are listening to Burgoyne, to Cæsar, to Cleopatra, or to Joan of Arc. He uses historical facts and figures to point his own modern thoughts too glaringly to let us forget the author for a moment. It is impossible to read his historical plays without remembering all the time that you are reading the work of the author of innumerable prefaces preaching the Vanity of Revenge and Punishment, the cruelty of prisons, and the wisdom of the words of Jesus 'Judge not and you be not judged'. In the stories of Cæsar and Cleopatra and Saint Joan (not to mention The Devil's Disciple) he found such good opportunities to dramatise these particular views that in the case of the former he has made the Vanity of Revenge and Punishment supply the theme for the most dramatic moment in his Cæsar's life, while in the case of the latter the cruelty of solitary imprisonment is flashed into the flaming light of drama at the climax of the Maid's Tragedy.

It is therefore very difficult to forget the author when listening to Cæsar. It is not Cæsar who stands up before his followers while the enemy is knocking at the gate and shouts 'These knockers at your gate are also believers in vengeance and in stabbing. You have slain their leader: it is right that they shall slay you . . .' — but Bernard Shaw uttering an unheeded warning against the Great War. It is not Cæsar who congratulates Rufio on cutting the throat of Ftatateeta without malice, without judgment, without indignation, without moralising — but Bernard Shaw the immoralist. And we never quite feel at ease with Joan. At one moment she is a peasant girl, at another a pure 'Shaw woman' who calls everyone by their nick and Christian names — is it more likely that a peasant girl in Feudal times would think it correct to call the Dauphin Charlie, than a peasant girl in our own time would think it correct to call the King, Georgie? At one moment she is naïve and simple, at another intellectual and cunning.

As a proof of how hard Shaw finds it to enter into the character of an historic figure without also projecting himself too obviously I would offer his constructive remarks upon Shakespeare in the Preface to the *Dark Lady of the Sonnets* — (not his supposedly destructive remarks in *Dramatic Essays*). I choose his remarks on Shakespeare, though the Jesus in *Androcles*, who is made out to be a faithful follower of Bernard Shaw, furnishes nearly as good an example of this trait. His reflections are interesting and illuminating, but the Shakespeare in whom he would have us believe is impossible. Religious history shows us how all men have always made God in their own image – so long as He was in the sky. The history of literature shows us how the critics of Shakespeare have likewise made *him* in their own image. As a critic of Shakespeare Shaw is no exception. 'I am convinced,' he writes, 'that Shakespeare was exactly like myself.' I cannot do justice to this remark. It will be sufficient to say that such a conviction is interesting rather than convincing. It is true that Shaw breathes new life into the rotting bones of ancient men but when they rise in glorious resurrection they have indeed been born again!

Occasionally he will permit a character to be nothing but a foil against an important character. Thus we get Brittanus existing with apparently no other purpose than to help us to understand Cæsar, and Octavius to help us to understand Tanner. At a stretch we are prepared to believe that Octavius' remarks to Tanner (so convenient for the author) are not out of character if he is supposed to be an imbecile, but when we are told that he is a poet, a close friend of Tanner, and a potential playwright, he becomes a monstrous absurdity, an insult to the reader.

Finally he creates characters such as Keegan, Undershaft, Marchbanks, the Statue, and the Devil who are less real than stimulating. Nevertheless it is astonishing how alive these people are in spite of the fact that what they say is of more importance than themselves. 'Stop making speeches, Andrew,' says Lady Britomart to Undershaft. 'I have to make speeches, my dear. It is my only way of making myself understood' — and so he gains our affections at once. Keegan is simply too good to be true. In spite of the immense length of the speeches in the Dream in *Man and Superman* we are left with a very definite impression of the character of the Devil and the Statue — though it must be admitted that Anne is but the shadow of a shade. I put Marchbanks in this final category because he appears to me to be at once too conventional and too unconventional. But poets, as a general rule, are not like that. They are nearly always more practical, abler, and more business-like than business men — and often better at games than their fellows. And in proportion as they are poetical so in proportion are they business-like. That is why Byron always consulted Shelley on all practical matters, that is why Browning had to look after Carlyle when travelling to the Continent, that is why (I borrow from Mr. Chesterton) if Shakespeare held horses in his early days it was because he was the best person to hold horses.[1]

[1]"This is true; but Marchbanks is fiercely practical, and obviously, as Candida sees, the stronger of the two. But this is quite compatible with his De Quinceyish shyness — or my own. De Quincey, by the way, starved for a week with a seven-day bill in his pocket, not knowing that he could discount it.' G. B. S. De Quincey is of course the one great exception to this general rule. J. S. C.

I will add that I would not sacrifice a word of Keegan and Undershaft or any of the Shaw eccentrics in the cause of reality. If we do not complain against the poorness of Shakespeare's men of action or the sameness of his heroines since they are the instruments of such poetry, neither should we complain against the creations of Shaw since their words flash into such eloquence and rise to such beauty. But I would go further than this. I would ask why we are so particular about a dramatist always staging our exact selves? We have only got to go out into the street to be surrounded by millions of people like ourselves, but we have got to go a long way before we can find conversation such as cometh from the pens of those whom God inspires. We are fond of saying that the first duty of a dramatist is 'to hold the mirror up to Nature'. I do not know what Shakespeare meant by that phrase but I do know what we mean by it. We mean that the first duty of a dramatist is to hold the mirror up to ourselves. Not to the animals, not to the flowers, not to the birds — but to ourselves. Not as we have been, not as we may be, not as we might be — but as we are. So frightful is this egomania, so blind are we to the pitiful picture which we present, that we insist that 'human nature never changes'. In an earlier chapter I tried to point out that (if we allow the term at all) we must realise that it never does anything else. Life, of which we are a part, will continue to change in spite of all our egotism and all our cant and all our lies. It is therefore one of the duties of a dramatist to paint not only pictures of ourselves but to give us visions of our future selves. So let us drop telling the dramatist that he must only hold up a mirror to ourselves and recognise that his work by no means ends there. Let us drop saying politely that *Back to Methuselah* 'passes practically out of the domain of drama' and recognise that a mirror held up to the mighty procession of life is the highest kind of drama we can possibly have. Let us recognise the fact that the proper study of mankind is not man, but Superman.

III

At present it is thought that perhaps the less said about Shaw's technique the better. There seems to be general bewilderment on the subject. We have Critics like M. Hamon insisting that Shaw is the English Molière and that his school of technique will become classic in France. We have Bernard Shaw himself telling us that when he is not sticking to the style of the Classics he is, as Hamon suggests, following the manner of Molière. We have on the other hand Mr. William Archer and all he stands for fiercely denouncing any similitude between Shaw and the Classics and insisting that his technique beside theirs is as a jelly-fish compared to a racehorse. Technique can be a dull and unprofitable subject. But I am confident that the reader may not find it altogether dull or unprofitable – especially if he is a-play-is-not-a-play person – to glance at the facts in Bernard Shaw's case.

It may seem difficult at first to see any resemblance between the technique of a Shaw play and that of a Molière play. Shaw is so bent on realism that he never forces the reader to remember that he is reading a play by giving a list of dramatis personæ at the beginning, by dividing his Acts into frequent scenes, by sudden stage directions in the middle of the action such as 'X comes in on right' or 'goes off left' or 'walks across stage', by writing 'curtain' at the end of an Act, by putting Lady B. instead of Lady Britomart, or by any of those little jerks which are so irritating in the plays of Oscar Wilde, Galsworthy, Synge and (sometimes) Barrie. He is so bent on clearness in his character-drawing that he gives a careful physical and psychological description of each character as he or she appears, which few will deny is a very welcome contrast to a Tolstoy or Tchekov play the difficulties of which in this way are so great as to force the reader to turn again and again to the beginning in order to find out who is speaking. It is therefore surprising at first to hear Shaw protesting that he sticks close to the manner of Molière who makes no attempt to conciliate the reader in any of these ways.

But a closer study shows us that the superficial differences are unimportant compared with the true resemblances between them. Comparisons are stupid things leading nowhere as a rule: I do not wish to compare the two writers but only by bringing them together for a moment to show the existence of a certain form of technique. Negatively they resemble one another in that they do not write 'well constructed' plays with a proper beginning, middle, and end, with a good expositive climax and *dénouement*. Positively both desire by the Spirit of Comedy to give a piece of life rather than to tell a story and to have conversation rather than material action. When Comedy reaches a certain height of inspiration it takes much the same form. *Le Misanthrope* may be called a play in the French manner, *The Cherry Orchard* may be called a play in the Russian manner, *John Bull's Other Island* may be called a play in the Shavian manner — but is there any real difference in their method? They are all High Comedy: that is to say, intensely tragic. The words and actions of the characters mean more than meets the eye. The plot, if there is one, is only there to serve the theme. Where they all differ from a Pinero or Henry Arthur Jones play they all resemble one another.

What precisely is meant by a Pinero play? The answer is important because it gives the clue to Mr. William Archer's inability to appreciate a play like *Heartbreak House* or *Back to Methuselah*. By a Pinero play is simply meant a good play, a strong drama. A story is told, and told well. The dramatist considers that his first duty is to tell a story, his second duty is to tell a story, his third duty is to tell a story.[1] (Those acquainted with Shaw's character can scarcely doubt that he therefore considered it to be his supreme duty never to tell a story.) In writing a Pinero play the dramatist must have good entrances and exits – that is to say everyone will come into the room for a good reason and go out for a reason which he is careful to state. He must have good 'curtains' – those enjoyable, easily conceived, unreal touches. He must finish his play (or game of chess) properly with an embrace, a suicide or a sudden surprise.

Now only a foolish man would sneer at such technique, for it is more or less the same technique as that adopted by many great dramatists whose aims were different. Sometimes this kind of technique was a splendid instrument in the hands of Shakespeare whose chief desire was to sing; in the hands of Ibsen whose chief aim was the pointing of a moral by Tragedy; and so there is no

---

[1] "It would be more correct to say that his first duty is to invent a situation, his second to lead up to it, and his third to get out of it as best he can. He begins with the end of Act II and goes on to Act I and Act III the latter being the most likely to be a makeshift. I am assuming that you are referring to the Proficient Playwright in general of the mid-nineteenth-century Parisian school. But the formula applies to the *Merchant of Venice* and to many of my own plays.' G. B. S.

reason why it should not be a splendid instrument in the hands of a Pinero whose chief aim is to entertain. But it is a technique which is not suitable for a genius of the Shaw-Molière-Tchekov type.

But critics like Mr. Archer who at bottom don't like anything that is not perfectly straightforward mislead the public into thinking that because Shaw's plays are not constructed in the Pinero manner, they are therefore badly constructed. In his brilliant book *The Old Drama and the New* (in which he attacks the foolish criticism of Modern Drama like Ruskin attacked the criticism of the Modern Painting of his generation) he tells us that Shaw's technique compared to that of the Classics is in the relation of a jelly-fish to a racehorse.

To answer convincingly this remarkable assertion would take a volume. This book is not on technique. I cannot therefore hope to persuade the reader that we have a master of compression in Mr. Shaw. I can only invite him to look closely at one Act of one play as an example and then having looked at all the other plays with equal scrutiny by himself, to decide how long we ought to tolerate this nonsense about Shaw's 'sloppy' technique.

Let us look at *Major Barbara*, Act II. The spectator finds himself looking into a Salvation Army shelter and in a few moments is familiar with Peter Shirley an honest poor man, Rummy a fallen woman, Snobby Price a cunning cockney, and Bill Walker a fairly commonplace ruffian. The first three have been 'saved', but Bill has come to drag back his girl who has joined the Salvation Army. A few minutes' conversation reveals each person's attitude towards the Salvation Army, towards their employers and towards life in general, and especially brings out their lack of sympathy for one another – a fact overlooked by many idealists. Jenny Hill, a Salvation Army girl, comes in and Bill roughly demands where his girl is. Finding himself opposed by everyone he strikes Rummy in the face and Jenny Hill on the jaw and indulges in a violent conversation with Peter Shirley who intimidates him by challenging him to fight Todger Fairmile the famous converted wrestler, and frightens him by revealing that the major of the shelter is the Earl of Stevenage's granddaughter and therefore a legally dangerous person.

All this which tells so much, suggests so much, and prepares so much, takes but eight pages of reading and ten minutes of hearing.

Then Major Barbara appears and begins to make Bill feel very uncomfortable at having hit Jenny Hill on the jaw; for by the method of showing concern for his soul but not anger or desire for revenge and punishment she makes his conscience begin to work – though he feels no pangs of conscience for having hit Rummy whom he knows is prepared to hit him back if she gets a chance. He feels the need of expiation for his guilt – being unaware that the accounts of the conscience cannot be settled by any sort of payment and that what is done can only be undone by the individual changing or, as the Bible has it, being born again. He feels the need for expiation so badly that he decides to get *his* face bashed in by Todger Fairmile. Thus hoping to make things square he departs to find the wrestler.

Meanwhile Undershaft and Cusins have come in and some very close conversation follows in which Undershaft proclaims that the two things necessary to Salvation are Money and Gunpowder. Then on the reappearance of Barbara a conversation arises in which the appalling state of the Army's finance is brought into tragic relief. At this point Bill comes back again. He is thoroughly depressed because so far from having got his face bashed in by Todger Fairmile, he has only succeeded in being quietly laid on his back by the converted wrestler who thereupon began to pray for him accompanied by the benedictions of the pious and the laughter of the profane. He has failed to square matters with Jenny Hill. What is he to do? How is he to soothe his conscience? He thinks of another way. He will pay cash for it. He produces a sovereign and offers it to Jenny Hill. But Barbara will not let her take it. It is clear to her that Bill cannot thus buy his Salvation. He must change or still be tortured by a troubled conscience. She will not take the blood-money; no, not even in order to use it to clothe the ragged or to cheer the desolate. So Bill with a sullen take-it-or-leave-it air throws the sovereign on the drum and relapses into silence.

Thus with a few dramatic strokes the whole fallacy of redemption, the vanity of punishment, and the accounts of conscience are brought before us into the lively regions of reality. Crosstianity is placed over against Christianity. Saint Paul is pilloried. And we can understand the language of Mr. W. T. Stead concerning it — 'Since I saw the Passion Play at Ober-Ammergau I have not seen any play which represented so vividly the pathos of Gethsemane, the tragedy of Calvary.' It might be thought that this would make sufficient matter for one act of one play. But no, Bill's placing a sovereign on the table serves more purposes than one.

For Mrs. Baines, a Salvation Army Commissioner, comes in joyfully with a tale of how Lord Saxmundham has promised to give £5000 to the Army if five other gentlemen will give £1000 each to make it up to ten thousand. She implores Undershaft to set the example by giving £1000 and at the same time indulges in a conversation with him which brief as it is paints her character with great plainness and also shows how the Salvation Army is strong by the bribe of bread and the bribe of Heaven, how it keeps down revolution and preserves the capitalist system, how it occupies much the same position as the Church in being an auxiliary police force, a 'chaplain on a pirate ship', or as Dean Inge has it 'a mere ambulance-corps'. Undershaft is quite willing to do so for the fun of making Lord Saxmundham pay up, and signs a cheque but at the same time tells them that their benefactor is really Sir Horace Bodger the distiller, famous for the Bodger's Whisky against which the Salvation Army has waged relentless war, and reminds them that his own money is made by supplying nations with weapons of destruction.

But Barbara who, unlike Mrs. Baines, has not been gifted with the great happiness that springs from stupidity, sees that if she will not allow Bill Walker to soothe his conscience by subscribing a pound neither ought she to allow Bodger to soothe his conscience (or buy salvation) by subscribing £5000. The others, however, who are ready to take the money for the Army from an evil source rather than no source at all, depart joyfully to a meeting, leaving the broken-hearted Barbara behind, to whom Bill now mockingly utters the phrase which illuminates the whole position of the Salvation Army – 'Wot prawce Selvytion nah?'

But that is not yet all – the pound which was placed on the drum has still a further part to play. For Bill looks round for it and finds it gone. He is furious. Rummy shouts from the window that she saw Snobby Price steal it as he went out – a saved man. He curses her for not having told him. She reminds him with imprecations that he had hit her in the face. He seizes a mug and flings it at her — which incident serves the purpose of intensifying the dramatic effect and of demonstrating the fact that Bill (who represents hundreds of thousands of men) 'without any change in his character whatsoever will react one way to one sort of treatment and another way to another'. He feels his conscience pricking him for having hit Jenny Hill because she has not retaliated: he feels no prickings of conscience for having hit Rummy because he knows that she is only too ready to retaliate.

I will concede to the reader that I have chosen this act for special considerations 'at random' — that is to say with care. But even if we admit that it is perhaps one of the best examples of Shaw's power of compression in the presenting of his ideas, what are we to think of a critic who implies that the man who can place the subtle psychological reactions of human nature under varying conditions, the tragedy of Calvary, the financial slavery of the Salvation Army, the strength and weakness of that Army, the vanity of revenge, the essential unity of life, and a dozen other points big enough to form the theme of a whole play, all within the compass of half an hour's attention, is a sloppy technician compared to a Pinero who devotes a whole play to centralising a stolen kiss? Shaw's technique is not that of a jellyfish but of a javelin. And I submit (without offering any proof) that whether we turn to the athletic straightforwardness of *Getting Married*, to the perfection of *Candida*, to the last Act of *Back to Methuselah* – especially the middle part in which a whole line of birds are knocked down with one stone – or to any other of the plays, we will find technique of a very high order.

Finally let me urge that there is no point in talking about 'the school of Bernard Shaw' as if he had inaugurated a movement. The movement has caused him not he the movement. He has consummated the rejuvenation of early twentieth-century drama just as Wagner consummated the wave of the nineteenth-century school of music, just as Pope consummated the wave of eighteenth-century 'correctness', just as Shakespeare consummated the Elizabethan wave of imagination, just as Euripides consummated the wave of rebellion against the Athenian Tradition, and just as Jesus of Nazareth consummated the wave of inspired prophecy. Breezy talk about 'the school of Bernard Shaw' and its likely effects in the future, is as silly as babbling about his 'early, middle and late periods'. Let us recognise that sort of criticism for what it is – a put-up job by which schoolboys and undergraduates pass examinations, Professors attain dignity and penmen make money.

IV

Let me now try and clear up the cardinal difficulty about *Major Barbara* and then show the significance of *Heartbreak House*. *Major Barbara* taken as a whole is a very difficult play. No one has yet given a suitable explanation of its cardinal difficulty. In the Preface the author tells us that once we have grasped the necessity for money Andrew Undershaft's views will not perplex us in the least – 'unless indeed his constant sense that he is only the instrument of a Will or Life Force which uses him for purposes wider than his own, may puzzle you'. And we admit that it is as easy to understand Undershaft the Repudiator of Poverty as to understand St. Francis the Repudiator of Riches. We admit that it is easy to sympathise with Undershaft the Mystic if we are anti-Neo-Darwinians. But it is Undershaft III the Dealer in Death and Destruction who is so puzzling. The fact that Undershaft's profession is that of a dealer in death and destruction is not what worries people. What worries them is that he is proud of it. It is not a necessity born of hardship about which he would like to say as little as possible. It is an article of faith. His Creed is Money and Gunpowder – the two things necessary to Salvation. Everyone stumbles over this. Mr. Henry Duffin in his *Quintessence of Bernard Shaw* goes so far as to quote Cusin's estimation of Undershaft, 'you are an infernal old rascal', as an expression of the author's opinion of him. But that explanation will not stand scrutiny. If ever Shaw wrote a play to preach a doctrine it is *Major Barbara*; if ever he chose a character as a mouthpiece for his doctrine it is Undershaft. There can be no sort of doubt about this if the Preface is read carefully. And even if there was no Preface to tell us so, the voice of Undershaft is unmistakably the voice of Shaw. But it is a very confused affair and one can sympathise with Mr. Archer's verdict that 'In *Major Barbara*, notwithstanding the "First Aid for Critics" which Mr. Shaw so kindly supplies in his preface, I confess that the main line of doctrine entirely eludes me. I cannot help thinking that there are two main lines, which eventually cross each other, so that the trains of thought which run on them collide, to their mutual destruction.' Though there is no particular reason why a genius should know the meaning of his works I am unwilling to believe that Mr. Shaw is puzzled over the behaviour of Undershaft. On the contrary I am convinced that he has no doubt whatever as to the meaning of his gospel of death and destruction – so little doubt as to find it inconceivable that anyone should be puzzled by it.

It seems to me that he wishes to illustrate a large number of points through Undershaft. The first point is one with which Undershaft himself would not agree. In the preface he points out how Froissart's knight considered that 'to rob and pill was a good life'. By which he meant that if the only way of obtaining a good life was by robbing and pilling he should rob and pill – though Mediaeval Society was to be strongly censored if that was the only way by which a man could obtain a good life. Shaw heartily agrees with Froissart's knight. Mrs. Warren's defence and Cashel Byron's defence for their respective professions are precisely the same as the knight's defence of his. So keen is Shaw upon this point that not content with showing it by a drama on Mrs. Warren's profession and by a novel on Cashel Byron's profession he drives it home again under cover of Undershaft's profession. So that in the end the reader cannot mistake the doctrine – wildly extravagant even for Bernard Shaw – that poverty is the vilest and blackest of sins, viler than prostitution, viler than prize-fighting, viler than murder.

This however is only part of the explanation of Undershaft the Dealer in Death and Destruction – an explanation with which he himself would not for a moment agree. He says to Cusins with all the enthusiasm of an Evangelist 'I shall hand on my torch to my daughter. She shall make my converts and preach my gospel' – the two things necessary to Salvation – 'Money and Gunpowder; freedom and power; command of life and command of death.'

That brings us up against a fact about Bernard

Shaw which is insufficiently understood at present. He is not afraid of killing as a test of sincerity. I must again remind the reader of his essay entitled *The Dictatorship of the Proletariat* in which he urges that if a man will not pay back his debt to the community by working for two hours a day there is only one thing to be done with him — namely to shoot him apologetically as an undesirable person. This preparedness to kill is, according to Undershaft, 'the final test of sincerity'. Thus Undershaft stands for much more than an individual person: he is a symbol of what the Government ought to be — an abolisher of poverty by means of holding a rifle to the heads of all those who refuse to work. He represents the man who is prepared to act instead of only talking.

In the preface Shaw points out quite truly that the French Revolution was caused not by the Encyclopedists, not by your Voltaires, Montesquieus, Rousseaus, (though I fancy he is hardly prepared to deny that they charged the air, so to write, with combustible matter) but by the common people who knew that they would perish unless they turned words into deeds. They knew that unless they personally set a match to the combustible air nothing would ever be done. They knew that the sword is mightier than the pen.

If we bear these political beliefs of Shaw in mind it becomes clear that the 'gunpowder' part of

Undershaft represents that readiness and power to act without which freedom (the 'money' part of Undershaft) is impossible to obtain. If we look at him in this light all his remarks – ironic or otherwise – take on an added significance. And as we leave the theatre we feel that he is indeed a hydra-headed villain (or hero) who stands for many things and teaches many doctrines. He stands as a symbol of the Repudiation of Poverty, as a symbol of a Servant of the Life Force, as a symbol of the complete Communist Government.

The difficulties in the understanding of this play are by no means made easier by the fact that Mr. Shaw was once a constitutional Fabian and therefore an anti-Undershaftian. It is surprising that he has not made himself clearer in his 'First Aid to Critics' for he knows as well as anyone that in such cases as this a genius is judged in the end by the things which he has left unsaid no less than by the things which he has said.

v

At the beginning of this book I gave the impression made on me when I saw *John Bull's Other Island* for the first time. *Heartbreak House* at the Court Theatre in 1921 seemed to me an equally glorious thing. I had read the play before rather hurriedly and had not been particularly struck by it. But now looking down on to the stage I was astonished at what was happening there. I was witnessing a battlefield of wit and wisdom. Everyone was hurling bombs at everyone else. It was an appalling sight: the frightful warfare of humanity was seen as if in a vision, the suffering seemed unspeakable, the comedy unrelenting. It was an inspiring sight: for at one period two were left alone in single combat — Hector and Shotover. They bent to their work: for five minutes they fought for Truth, they battled for Light, till you could see the very blood falling on the stage! The curtain dropped on the First Act. People looked at one another. I said to my companion: 'It is good for us to be here.'

I write the above impression because personal impressions from whatever source they come are valuable, and because I am convinced that many feel as I do about *Heartbreak House*. But the critics would have none of it. Oh no! it was hopelessly irregular, its plot was obscure, its technique was Russian, it was nothing but talk, talk, talk! Its meaning was not clear, it was destructive and we are 'tired of destructive criticism' and so on through pages of constructive criticism. In vain did enlightened persons write in protest against such a verdict of such a play; in vain did Mr. H. W. Massingham remind them that a man of genius feeling the great burden of his day must needs wrap up his message in a parable so that the scene of *Heartbreak House* was really no more in a country villa than the fiery mount up which

Siegfried fought his way was a spur of the Taunus or the Westerwald: in vain did Mr. A. G. Gardiner declare that never in the history of the drama had such an immense theme been brought so triumphantly within so small a compass; in vain did Mr. Graham Sutton implore his colleagues to remember that a fantasy in the Russian manner could hardly be expected to play like *The Second Mrs. Tanqueray*. It was no good: the critics had foully hit below the mental belt and the play was taken off before the public had time to forget them. It will be interesting to see how they have changed over by the time it is revived in the West End.

Can we make out the meaning of this great play? This being probably one of the most inspired of all his plays it is little use asking the author to explain it. After the second 'first night' of that play there was a tea party on the stage over which Mr. Shaw presided. He was asked at intervals what the play meant. 'How can I know?' he replied. 'I'm the author.' And he is fond of pointing out how often Wagner and Ibsen did not know what they meant. This need not surprise us, for on reflection it is obvious that a genius when fully inspired is at the mercy of something other and greater than himself. At such moments, to use colloquial language, he trusts to luck that what he is writing means something. In order to meet this difficulty we invented the art of criticism – the business of the critic being to find out what the author means. Unhappily criticism is too often sullied by men who criticise without knowledge, without dignity, without honour and without fairness.

So we must not expect to gather much about the play from the preface. Indeed his prefaces seldom explain the plays. They lead up to them, that is all.[1] When he gets to a certain point in his subject he employs a new vehicle – drama – in order that he may conduct the reader into regions denied to mere straightforward prose. It is odd that Mr. Shaw should be looked upon by so many people as a man who is always explaining himself. The fact is he never explains the best part of himself. Thus all the help he gives us in the preface in question is to tell us that *Heartbreak House* 'is cultured, leisured Europe before the war', and then leaves us to wonder why he calls it a fantasy in the Russian manner on *English Themes*.

Before going on to endeavour to pull the sym-

---

[1] 'Really the play leads up to the preface so far as there is any leading up in the matter at all. . . . The prefaces are wholly independent of the plays, and are mostly written long after the play has been produced on the stage. The monumental preface to a volume of plays is a classic English tradition coming down from Ben Jonson in the Folio through Dryden, Rowe, etc., and the notion that such prefaces are intended to be read by the audience before the curtain rises is partly ignorance of literary history and partly mere native imbecility.' G. B. S.

bolic meaning of the play into some sort of shape I shall be permitted to apologise for doing so. For it is as easy to say too much about a play of this nature as it is to say too little. To write pages of abstract thought upon the meaning of a great play or a great picture is the worst form of literary trifling. It is destructive to the happiness of mankind. No one can bear to look at the Monna Lisa after having read Walter Pater's account of it. In the middle of the London season it is impossible to fill the New Oxford Theatre to witness a performance of *Hamlet* because that play is so charged with the philosophy of its critics. Anyone can make anything mean what he wants it to mean: anyone can twist the truth about to make a trap for fools. I merely make the following extremely fallible suggestions because I am in violent reaction against those people who can see nothing in *Heartbreak House* but 'a delightful evening's entertainment in which you laugh all the time'.

It is a parable – worthy of the author who is always reminding us that 'in real life truth is revealed by parables and falsehood supported by facts'. But we must remember Shaw's own words in *The Perfect Wagnerite*, 'do not forget that an allegory is never quite consistent except when it is written by some one without dramatic faculty, in which case it is unreadable'. The reason for this is that the only way to dramatise an idea is by putting on the stage living creatures possessed with that idea. That may lead the writer into difficulties: but a glance at Bunyan compared with Ben Jonson or at Shaw compared with a purely 'expressionistic' play is sufficient to show the necessity of not stageing abstractions. We take less pleasure in seeing Patriotism on the stage than a patriotic man.

Thus in *Heartbreak House* it is a mistake to think that every scene, every remark, and every person symbolises some universal scene, applies to all the world, and incarnates a world type of person. It seems to me that at moments it is just a scene in a country house in England and that the remarks and the people are entirely local, but that at other times the local character is altogether in the background and the House becomes the ship of Europe dashing on the rocks filled with foolish people jazzing down to death.

Let us look at the chief characters. Mangan is of course the symbol of commercialism, industrialism, big business, finance. His money gives him power to rule over and ruin other men and yet he is not happy since he cannot buy love or respect or honour from the people who consort with him only for the sake of his money. Upon the significance of his grateful victim Mazzini Dunn, I need not enlarge. Randall the Rotter stands for that large class of men who seem to have nothing to do except to be tormented by women. Hector stands for that class of men (more in evidence before the war, when the play was written) who can find no suitable outlet for their brains and waste their energies in philandering and telling lies. By what right he has to speak so oracularly in Act I, I am unable to say.

Though Ellie Dunn is a splendidly human figure, though she is a typical example of the girl whose heart is broken amongst the leisured classes, though her cry 'This is the end of happiness and the beginning of peace' comes from the single heart, she seems nevertheless to be something more than Ellie Dunn. She seems to be the soul of Europe at the mercy of Hector's lies; at the mercy of Mangan's money. When later on she has to choose between selling herself to Mangan and facing the world with 'her strong sound soul' and the company of Captain Shotover, we feel that it is Europe's choice. And when she cries 'Now I know the real reason why I couldn't marry Mr. Mangan: there would be no blessing on our marriage. There is a blessing on my broken heart: there is a blessing on your beauty, Hesione. There is a blessing on your father's spirit. Even on the lies of Marcus there is a blessing; but on Mr. Mangan's money there is none' – we feel inexpressively relieved though the meaning may be doubtful.

Hesione does not appear to me to have any particular significance other than as a typical charming woman who is not quite so intelligent as she seems. Lady Utterword is what her name perhaps implies – commanding respectability incarnate. Unfortunately she is afraid of facing facts, with the result that she cannot understand her own heart[1] (remember her rage when Ellie mentioned that organ) or the foundations upon which the House rests (remember her simple remedy for all its ills).

The burglar is an interesting figure. He is thrown in partly to make the fantasia the more fantastic, partly to demonstrate the flimsiness of *Heartbreak House*, partly to give rein to the Spirit of Comedy, and partly to illustrate a fact about prisons which the author has very much at heart. Amongst the many arguments which he uses, in his preface to Mr. and Mrs. Sidney Webb's book on Prisons, to show that one of the aims of prisons – deterrence – does not deter, is the argument that statistics by no means show all the crimes actually committed. 'For', he writes, 'it is the greatest mistake to suppose that everyone who is robbed runs to the police: on the contrary only foolish or ignorant or very angry people do so without serious consideration and great reluctance. In most cases it costs nothing to let the thief off and a good deal to prosecute him. The burglar in *Heartbreak House* who makes his living by robbing people, and then blackmailing them by threatening to give himself up to the police and put

[1] 'She hasn't got one and wants one dreadfully.' G.B.S.

them to the expense and discomfort of attending his trial and giving evidence after enduring all the worry of the police enquiries, is not a joke: he is a comic dramatisation of a process that is going on every day.'

Finally what shall we say of Captain Shotover? He presents no problem. He is simply the voice that crieth in the wilderness – the voice that is not heard.

In spite of the symbolism of these characters the meaning of Acts I and II can hardly be put on paper. Everything is confused. Perhaps that is the point. Perhaps the critics are unconsciously right: it is a question of talk, talk, talk, and nothing done, symbolic of pre-war Europe! Europe before the war was a place of heartbreak, wrangling, confusion, and the laughter of lunatics. In Act III however a sinister change comes about in the drama. We feel that something is going to happen. At first, joining in the spirit of this tempestuous drama we, so to write, stray and stumble not quite knowing where we are; but as the play advances the vision of life begins to be seen more clearly through the mist and we are borne on relentlessly towards a disaster that seems to threaten all the world. We hear the distant drumming in the sky, prophetic of some coming crash. We hear the complaints concerning the foundations of the House by its inhabitants, prophetic of some coming doom: we hear the remarks of Mazzini Dunn, symbolic of the men who always say 'Oh nothing will happen, nothing ever happens; we will muddle through all right'; we hear the voice of Hector raised in protest against himself and his companions, symbolic of the man who can do but does not, we hear the warning words of Shotover suddenly breaking into wild excitement — and then, crash! The end has come. The German bomb has fallen, symbolic of the bomb that fell upon every nation in Europe, symbolic of the blow that Nature strikes after sitting for generations on her stile watching the follies of mankind.

Then we watch what happens — the actions of each character. Hector the talker, the idler, is transformed. Someone puts the light out: he is furious. 'Who put that light out?' he cries. 'Who dared put that light out!?' Nurse Guiness complains that it can be seen for miles: 'It shall be seen for a hundred miles!' he shouts and dashes into the house to switch on all the lights and tear down all the curtains. Lady Utterword faces the disaster with all the intrepidity and courage of the refined while Randall implores her to go down into the cellar. It is announced that the first bomb has demolished the rector's house. 'The Church is on the rocks, breaking up,' cries Captain Shotover. 'I told him it would unless it headed for God's open sea:' — (remember the Church at the beginning of the war: how Jesus was re-sold in every cathedral and re-crucified at every Altar). Another explosion! Mangan — the practical commercial man useless in war time — is killed: the burglar is killed. The danger passes. And Ellie has gained courage and spirit from the ordeal.

CHAPTER NINE

Common Sense about Shaw's Workmanship: The Narrator we have Lost

*

I

THE history of Style from the Victorian age to this age is interesting. During the last century style was looked upon as a vastly important thing. Men like Robert Louis Stevenson came forward saying that style was something that had to be formed before a man's writings could be of any value; men like Oscar Wilde came along advocating style for style's sake and attacking those who used it to carry a message or preach a gospel; and finally long essays and even whole books on the subject were published to the delight of the public and the profit of the authors. Those were great days for all who had nothing to say but said it very beautifully. And Literary Criticism flourished splendidly in the midst of the garden.

The inevitable reaction has already set in with such violence that it is difficult to find any upholder of style. This reaction began with the late Samuel Butler who expressed his desire to put it on record that 'I never took the smallest pains with my style, have never thought about it and do not know whether it is a style or whether it is not, as I believe and hope just common straightforwardness.' Then as the century advanced came Mr. Bernard Shaw who declared that he would not undergo the toil of writing a single sentence for Art's sake alone; came Mr. H. G. Wells who declared that he did not want to be a man of letters but a journalist; came Mr. Arnold Bennett who told us that a man's style was no more and no less than a man's thoughts; came Mr. Hilaire Belloc who said that it was often necessary in the interests of lucidity to split an infinitive, and sometimes in the interests of emphasis to begin a sentence with 'and' or to end it with 'of' — until the Belles-Lettres gentlemen seemed sadly out of countenance!

But to state this modern view is not to praise it.

It is one thing to complain against the pedant who says that you can't in the interest of good style (when you *must* sometimes in the interests of lucidity) begin a sentence with 'and'; who says that you can't with propriety use 'people' when you should use 'persons'; who says that to use 'which' when you should use 'that,' or to write 'one' when you should write 'you' is to betray a trust. But it is quite another thing to complain against the man who says that you should take trouble over your style. In a recent number of *The Nation* Mr. Leonard Woolf defended himself against the appalling charge of having mentioned the importance of style, in these words referring to Joseph Conrad — 'He belonged to the high and ancient tradition of the literary artist, of that strange and rare succession of men who do not care to fling out a bare thought anyhow for Tom, Dick, or Harry to make their own.'

I venture to suggest that those words admirably

express a too long neglected sentiment. But I would go further than this. I would say that it is the business of a man of letters to do the best he can for his readers. He has no right to put his thoughts down on paper until he has decided the best possible way to put them there. It is his business to wrestle ruthlessly with the unwilling words until his thought is clean and his rhythm pure. It is his business to make the best use he can of the weapons which have been forged for him in the fires of Time. He must have a good reason for it if he would depreciate the uses of the comma, the gifts of the semi-colon, the powers of the colon and the dash in keeping a long sentence straight and clean. If a man of letters does not appreciate these things and a thousand other such things besides; if he is not prepared to drive the awkward and ugly phrase off his page altogether, I know not how he can be considered faithful to his calling.

This need not always apply. Carlyle simply could not write at all in the ordinary way, but his style (at a price) owing to the ragged and jagged thoughts of the great man, attains a rough, rude beauty of its own. Bunyan, caring nothing for literature or style or drama but only for the Pilgrim's journey and the Celestial City, had all these things added unto him. But unless we feel that we are even as these two, we can hardly allow ourselves so much license.

Now let us turn to Bernard Shaw. It is true that

he made the often quoted remark 'I would not undergo the toil of writing a single sentence for Art's sake alone.' It is also true that he made the less well known remark 'I never have to think how to say anything in prose: the words come with the thought. I often have to argue a thing carefully to get it right; but when I have found the right thing to say it says itself instantly; and matters of feeling don't even have to be argued ... I always tell people that if they can't do three quarters of any art by nature they'd better sweep a crossing.' But along with those remarks should be remembered his constant easy talk about his 'rather exceptional literary knack cultivated by dogged practice', his declaration that his *Saturday Review* career gave him the impetus to form his style, and his statement to his biographer that he 'believes in style'. And along with these remarks must be taken the fact that he cares enormously for Art and is – like Ruskin – first and foremost an artist but was – for the same reason as Ruskin – compelled to turn his attention to other things.

It is important that we should get clear on this point. Nothing is more ludicrous than to hear people who have snatched a passing acquaintance with perhaps one of the arts reproach Shaw for caring so little about Art and preferring Socialism instead – Shaw if you please, the specialist in Music, the man who resigned his post of Art-critic to the *World* because he was asked to degrade the dignity of his profession, the man who in all Europe was alone found competent to deal with the charge of Degeneracy brought against all the arts by Max Nordau, the man whose chief failing as a novel writer was his employment of a too stylish style, the man who is always praising 'that passion for efficiency which is the true master-passion of the artist', the man who in all his novels and in half his plays reflects enthusiastically upon the everlasting warfare which the artist wages against anything and everything that conflicts with his desire to create. If everyone cared a quarter as much about Art as Mr. Shaw there would probably be no need for Shaw the Socialist.

Mr. Shaw's position and attitude in this matter can be best explained by turning for a moment to the Art for Art's Sake controversy. It is a controversy only surpassed in futility by its two sisters — The Battle of the Books in the days of Swift, and the question concerning the Dramatic Unities over whose tomb some critics continue to weep. The futility, not to say sterility, of the Art for Art's Sake controversy lies in the fact that whichever side you take you exclude from literature a long list of great names. Thus if you say that literature should only be written for a moral purpose you exclude men like Shakespeare and Keats, and if you say it should be written only for its own sake you exclude men like Swift and Bunyan. It is not a subject that can be argued. It is a question of humanity. Art is for the sake of us all. We can only enjoy it when we are not hungry. But millions of us are hungry or are so busy trying to make enough money to keep us from being hungry that we have no time for Art. What kind of men are best fitted to make suggestions for the improving of such a dreadful situation? The men with the best and freest intellects – who very often are the great literary artists. If these artists care for humanity they will therefore bend all their literary power for the purpose of improvement rather than pleasure. Thus we find men like Ruskin and Morris and Shaw each in their different ways starting their careers as artists pure and simple and then after a brief period of contact with the real world we see them plunge into political economy.

Can anyone pretend to be glad of this? Is not the deep misery of these modern days symbolised by the fact that great artists and poets like Shaw and Ruskin and Morris are forced to make Art their recreation and political agitation their life work? Think of all the masterpieces Shaw might have written had he not spent half his life in the dry drudgery of getting up facts for the platform and the ephemeral pamphlet – facts which are only used so that they may be meaningless to posterity. Shaw knows that in Utopia, if it ever dawns, Art will in a broad sense be carried on for its own sake and will never be used in the service of politics. For to the stranger travelling in any future Utopia who asks 'how do you manage here as regards politics?' the reply shall always be given as it was given to the stranger in Morris's *News From Nowhere*, 'we get on excellently because we have none'. In Utopia there will be one subject unheard of – politics: one class of men unknown – politicians.

But because Shaw has over-emphasised the importance of Art only as a moral force it is concluded that he considers style of no account, – a very pleasant thought for all those who cannot write. That is why I make the following remarks, by no means all complimentary, as regards his workmanship which is supposed not to exist. I prefer to use the word workmanship rather than style. Style is another of those words which can mean anything. Ruskin and Carlyle, Walter Pater and De Quincey, Samuel Butler and Macaulay, Stevenson and Gibbon, Froude and Dr. Johnson, have all, to my certain knowledge, been called by reputable critics Masters of Prose Style. I do not complain of this: it is probably all right: it confuses me a little, that is all. So I prefer to speak of Shaw's workmanship.

Like Francis Bacon he employs three different ways of writing. Just as Bacon had one way for his essays, another for his scientific work and a third for his *New Atlantis* (I recommend this fact to Baconians, for if he employed three manners why should he not have employed a fourth manner in order to write Shakespearian plays?), so

Bernard Shaw employs one way of writing for his prefaces, another for his plays, and a third for his mysticism.

In order to enjoy reading his prefaces it is necessary to learn his preface manner. It is often just as necessary to learn a writer's 'style' as it is to learn a foreign language. If you are a good linguist in this way your literary travels will be Catholic. It is absolutely necessary to learn Carlylian: and it is to a lesser degree necessary to learn Shavian – for the prefaces.

His purpose in the prefaces is to fit all he has to say into a comparatively short space. And he has a desperate amount of things to say and facts to place. He has therefore made a remarkable vehicle to carry his goods. Its chief characteristic is celerity. The reader is hurled along at a pace such as he has never before experienced during all his literary travels. Take the following passage: – 'We shall continue to maintain the White Slave Trade and protect its exploiters by, on the one hand, tolerating the white slave as the necessary breakwater of marriage; and on the other, trampling on her and degrading her until she has nothing to hope from our Courts; and so with policemen at every corner, and law triumphant all over Europe, she will still be smuggled and cattle-driven from one end of the civilised world to the other, cheated, beaten, bullied, and hunted into the streets to disgusting overwork, without daring to utter the cry that brings, not rescue, but exposure and infamy, yet revenging herself terribly in the end by scattering blindness and sterility, pain and disfigurement, insanity and death among us with the certainty that we are much too pious and genteel to allow such things to be mentioned with a view to saving either her or ourselves from them.'

The reader can count for himself the number of ideas and facts with which that one sentence is charged. It will be seen that in order to say all that he thinks necessary, he has to employ drastic measures. It means the using of gigantic sentences and the sweeping away of paragraphs; it means the ruthless extermination of the scorching adjective by which Ruskin burns his way into our hearts; and it means practically throwing over the semi-colon altogether and promoting the comma into a position which its powers are inadequate to justify. Some like this new literary vehicle, some hate it; some are fascinated by its celerity, others find it impossible – except when they are feeling very well. It is very good or very bad according to taste. But such a method of writing has also two grave disadvantages. First, it makes the reader go quickly when he ought to go slowly. It is impossible to catch more than a third of what a Shavian sentence is conveying on the first reading. The train goes too quickly through such wonderful country. It is necessary to go the journey several times. But few people will do this – which leads to the second disadvantage, namely that it is easy to think Shaw superficial. If you read sentences which are so arranged as to make you read very fast it is difficult to help feeling that the writer has written them very fast without taking much thought. That is the curse under which all writers who can write in a readable way fall. Simply because Samuel Butler wrote in a readable way about Evolution nobody took any notice of him: simply because Darwin wrote in an unreadable way everyone believed everything he said — though to this day much of what he really meant is absolutely obscured by vile tautologies. Had he realised that it was his duty as a citizen no less than as a man of science to write intelligently, the literary history of Evolution would have been saved many a painful chapter. But I suppose he knew, what all philosophers, all doctors, all scientists, all psychologists, all economists, and all theologians know, that to write unintelligibly is to attain honour and wealth and power.

It is necessary to add however, that another of the views of Shaw's preface-manner is that he *does* quite often become unintelligible. But not in an impressive way. Take this sentence from *Peace Conference Hints*: —

'That the national outputs of the belligerents have never been better distributed than during the war; that millions of labourers and their families have been better fed and clothed than ever in their lives before; that nevertheless colossal profits have been made by some employers, does not console the governing class for the reduction of its permanent incomes by more than one third through income tax and super-tax, for a fifty per cent. reduction in the purchasing power of the two thirds that remain, and for the threat of a levy on capital which though founded on the absurd delusion that the figures of the War Loans and Victory Loans and Liberty Loans are anything now but memoranda of claims for interest payable out of future production, may nevertheless have the effect of confiscating that interest, and forcing property holders to mortgage their estates and their industrial stocks and shares to the Government for nothing, as the Government will simply write off the amount of the mortgage against the "capital levy" which has compelled the victim to mortgage.'

To continue a useful metaphor this is a case of the vehicle going so fast that the passenger cannot help falling out. Ruskin or Macaulay would have recognised the necessity of employing regular punctuation in such a case but Shaw has deliberately flouted the full stop, expelled the colon, derided the semi-colon and mocked the comma with the result that it is not possible to reach the end of the sentence and retain its meaning. Such a sentence is mere playing with the reader. It is Shavian shorthand.

Finally he will sometimes defiantly fling pronouns in our face in a manner not to be tolerated. For instance he throws down the following very important remark in his preface to *Cashel Byron's Profession*: —

'At last I grew out of novel-writing, and set to work to find out what the world was really like. The result of my investigations, so far, entirely confirms the observation of Goethe as to the amazement, the incredulity, the moral shock with which the poet discovers that what he supposed to be the real world does not exist, and that men and women are made by their own fancies in the image of the imaginary creatures in his youthful fictions, only much stupider.'

He means, I take it, by that sentence that the intuitions of a poet are true and that men and women are unnatural. Badly as I have put it, I submit that Mr. Shaw could not have put it worse than he did.

Before turning away from this remarkable weapon in the Shavian armoury I would call attention to the 'monkey-gland' paragraph in the preface to *Saint Joan*. It is delightful. But no other man in Europe would have dared to throw down such a sentence.

So we come to his second method, which we find in the plays. All that need really be said about this prose is that it is magnificent. It is superb oratory. All actors revel in it — for in a sense all actors are orators just as all orators are actors. Actors love delivering Shavian passages because they are written and carefully punctuated for delivery by a man who knows exactly what the lips can do. I think that Shaw has gone as far with athletic prose as it is possible to go just as Shakespeare brought blank verse as far as it could go. There is a limit to these things — that is why Shaw always insists that in this way he is *not* greater than Shakespeare. Of course by writing in prose he gains tremendously over Shakespeare in so far as his plays act superbly while most of us who are fond of Shakespeare prefer to stay away from his theatre. But I suppose that that will always be the case with poetry. The moment Shaw's prose rises into poetry I am terrified of what the actor may do to it.

His plays are full of long passages of rhetoric and impassioned eloquence. For he understands the uses of rhetoric: he knows its power — (lucidity and rhetoric being Irish traits, outside Ireland). He knows that of all the shocking nonsense that is talked about 'style' nothing is more horrible in its deadly unreality than the silly jibes at rhetoric and the purple patch. He knows that there is no weapon in the literary armoury so useful for the economic placing of facts, marshalling of arguments, pointing of truths, and knitting of ideas, as rhetoric. He knows that it has faithfully served the highest moments of the great verse poets, and that though bad rhetoric is worse than bad anything else, appalling in its cruelty to reader or listener, good rhetoric is a great art and a noble instrument. A good example of exceptionally daring rhetoric is provided by Larry Doyle's famous outburst, and of exceptionally good eloquence by the Inca of Perusalem's one long outburst in the little playlet under that name. And I am convinced that far the best part of *Saint Joan* is the Tent scene. That is Shaw at his best, doing what he alone can do better than any other man alive or dead, namely dramatise a passionate and intellectual and religious conversation. It is not surprising therefore that the real acting triumph when *Saint Joan* was first acted fell not to the actress who played Joan but to the actor who played the Bishop of Beauvais. He demonstrated by performances of unassailable power what well-delivered Shavian oratory is really like.

As regards his third method of writing I have said all that needs saying on that score when dealing with him as a poet. I will only add with absolute conviction that such work is not born for death and that the closing lines of *Back to Methuselah* will endure long after marble and the gilded monuments of princes have perished from the earth.

I hope I have said enough to show that so far from Shaw being a careless writer and a mocker at art he cares so much for form that he has made three separate vehicles to carry his thought. Passing by his many interesting tricks (it is not my business to give them away) which he employs to force home his facts and ideas, it remains for me to point out one other important thing about his workmanship. I mean the amazingly high level he has always kept. He has never sunk below himself. He has never sold his pen. His journalism is written quite as carefully as any other part of his work.

Therefore much of his work is a superb example of the debt Literature owes to Journalism. In an interesting article in *The Observer* celebrating W. B. Yeats's reception of the Nobel Prize Mr. J. C. Squire drew attention to what he believed to be part of the greatness of Mr. Yeats — namely, that he never wrote Journalism. Surely there can only be one reply to this: we wish he had. A writer (if sincere and not pot-boiling) often throws off something in the heat of journalism which afterwards is prized as great literature. Journalism helps to keep a writer's name alive after he is dead. I recently read an old article by Mr. G. K. Chesterton written about 1906 and was astonished at its perfection. It seemed to me enormously better than much of his subsequent literature.

When Bernard Shaw wrote once a week for *The Saturday Review* he took extreme pains over each article, endeavouring to get to the bottom of everything he tackled. Nothing is less superficial than his journalism. Every paradox is a sermon, every epigram an illumination, every jest a judgment. The result is that some of the best pieces of literature he has ever written appeared first as journalism. I do not think that the opening paragraphs of his article in *The Saturday Review*, January 25th, 1896 on Church and Stage or his outburst in *The Nation*, March 19th, 1910 concerning the 'Elektra' of Strauss and Hoffmanstahl, have, with the exception of his mystic passages, ever been surpassed by anything else in all his work.

II

I never read Shaw for long without being infuriated at the thought of what a great Narrator we have lost in him. It is not from his novels that I get this feeling. They are all good reading but that is in spite of rather than because of the fact that they are novels. The parts which are most attractive in them are those occasions when the respective heroes rise to their feet and deliver long lectures on Socialism and Society and Art, and when the dialogue is sometimes as good as the dialogue in his plays. Perhaps I should say that we have lost not so much a Narrator as a marvellous Describer of persons and scenes. It is impossible to read his account of the wandering of H. W. Davies, or his description of the Carpentier-Becket fight ('Carpentier's face suddenly looked a hundred years old, his eyes saw through stone walls . . .'), or his description of the scene called Defying the Lightning in the preface to *Back to Methuselah*, or the précis of the Gospels in

Androcles, or his character sketches of his own creations in the plays, without a genuine feeling of disappointment that he has never given free scope to this remarkable talent.

It should be observed incidentally that the very people who generally complain that Shaw's characters are not real are also those who say that it 'is wrong' to describe characters so fully in mere stage directions. It is very hard to write, speak, or think quietly upon this small point. Which is the most ludicrous spectacle, the dramatist who writes insultingly clipped stage directions of which a ploughboy would be ashamed and then complains that the public will not read plays, or the public who turning from reading plays simply because of these very stage directions yet abuses the playwright who would doctor the situation? Shaw, thank God, answered the dramatist who said grandiloquently 'Quod scripsi, scripsi' with 'What you haven't written you haven't written. Which is a great pity.' Let those of us who want to see a play-reading public say simply and quietly to the man who declares that 'enter Lady B.' is good enough for him, that it is not good enough for us.

A long time ago Mr. Shaw said that he was sure he had not yet found out all his capacities and gifts. I suggest to him that he has underrated his descriptive talent and that if he can find time to write plays such as *Augustus Does His Bit* he could find time to exercise that talent. Let him finish as he began by writing five novels. I do not suggest that he should tell a story – such a thing is not to be thought of. I do not suggest that he should have a hero – though a novel with a hero would nowadays be a novelty. I merely suggest that for once he would not lecture, for once he would write a book describing people and places and things for description's sake. I guarantee the result.

CHAPTER TEN

Common Sense about Shaw's 'Originality'

★

COMPLETE originality of thought is now impossible. At least it is possible only as Robert Nicol has put it, 'for the hermit, the lunatic, or the sensational novelist'. That is why most great writers frankly own – like Byron – that their apparent originality is only some old idea brought forward again in a new way. We have been warned that it is a foolish thing to put new wine into old bottles but that must not blind us to the fact that modern originality chiefly consists of putting old wine into new bottles. The great writer nowadays is he who makes familiar things new rather than new things familiar. An idea has only got to become sufficiently old-fashioned to be modern.

But you may add that what the great genius also does is this: he goes further along the road to Truth than the genius who came before him. The track has already been discovered and trod by others but he goes a step further than any of them. And his successor goes still further than him. Bernard Shaw is a good example of this kind of originality. He has gone further with the theory of Creative Evolution than Samuel Butler or Bergson. He has wandered in the company of his Ancients through strange seas of thought, alone. Further than this he has logically followed up that Religion by steadily looking at the world from an immoral viewpoint. The result is that so far as originality goes nowadays he is certainly our most original and therefore most singular thinker.

If once therefore one can thus get an index to the mind of a man like Shaw it does not seem to me good sense to talk about his having 'cribbed' his philosophy from this or that person. It is his business to take what he can from the pool of thought to which all thinkers have contributed since the world began. And when one takes the matter in hand and looks closely it does not seem plain what he owes to the wonderful list of writers he is supposed to have cribbed. Nietzsche was once a name to conjure with but dates refute the assumption of the crib-finders. It would be a very remarkable thing if Nietzsche and Shaw were the only two exploiters of the extremely obvious superman idea in a world like this which hero-worships the strong. As a matter of fact they were not: Shaw's hero Michel Angelo was the first to think in those terms. To say that Shaw's ideas were taken from Ibsen is refuted by the publication of *The Irrational Knot* before *A Doll's House* was written. And why on earth should Shaw have taken anything from Ibsen whom he absurdly overrates?[1] A study of the two men's work inevit-

[1] 'I slummocked into almost thinking so myself until I re-read him for the final edition of my *Quintessence*; and then he got me again as powerfully as ever. It was he who made Shakespeare appear so shallow for the ten years following the arrival of his plays in England in 1889. He was a giant in dramatic literature. Take care not to class

ably produces that question — and I would add that the portrait of Ibsen that hangs in the gallery at Christiania appears to me to reveal the most unpleasant looking face I have ever seen: the mouth may be that of a strong man but it is certainly not the mouth of either a wise or great man. From Tolstoy he does not appear to me to have taken more than a hint as to how powerful a drama can be made out of a rough hand like Blanco Posnet, and as to how useful an open criticism of Shakespeare may be.[1] As regards Samuel Butler, apart from the fact that it is difficult to see how Shaw could owe Butler a greater debt than Butler owes Shaw, the methods of the two men and their general view of life are nearly as different as they could possibly be. But there is one man seldom mentioned in this connection who does appear to have had all Shaw's views before Shaw pronounced them to a very remarkable extent. I mean simply his friend William Morris. *News From Nowhere* is almost Bernard Shaw summar-

yourself with the pigmies who could see no higher than his boots.' G. B. S.

[1] 'Tolstoy's criticism of Shakespeare came my way long after my *Saturday Review* campaign. We corresponded about it; but we could not agree that the old Lear was better than Shakespeare's. However there is no need to cite Tolstoy. Voltaire and Dr. Johnson criticised him very freely. Neither Byron nor William Morris would bow the knee to Stratford. The bardolatry I shook up was simple ignorance: the bardolators never read him.' G. B. S.

ised. It contains Shaw's exact views on education, children, marriage, crime, punishment, and Communism — though of course it does not contain Shaw's philosophy. But if you want to find a book published in 1890, every word of which might have been written by the Bernard Shaw we know, turn to *News From Nowhere*. Also (though I am not competent to speak about music) I fancy he has gained far more from listening to Wagner and Mozart than he has gained from all his reading put together.[1]

But the point that I would make here is — that it does not matter. A man either has an original mind or he has not. The test is simple. In Boswell's Johnsonian Dialogues there is some talk between Beauclerk and Johnson concerning a third person who entertained pretensions to being a wit. 'I thought he *was* rather witty when I was introduced to him the other day,' said Beauclerk. 'Meet him again, Sir,' said Johnson. If you want to find out whether an author's thefts are really thefts or only open borrowings or mere coincidences, turn to his works in which no 'thefts' are possible and see if the same mind is behind it all. If you do that in the case of Bernard Shaw; if you turn to *Peace Conference Hints* or Preface to *Parents and Children* for instance and compare it with a piece supposed to be taken from someone else, you find exactly the same original mind at work.

[1] 'Hooray! . . .' G. B. S.

Moreover it is absurd to suppose that two writers do not often think of the same thing independently of one another. Nothing is more crucifying to the mind than to read literary criticism which selects two phrases from two widely different authors and then proceeds to say that one took the idea from the other. We all know the man who takes some senseless phrase from one of the Metaphysical Poets, from Donne or Cowley or Crashaw or Herbert or Hobington, some phrase such as 'I hear sweet intonations in the purling stream' and then proceeds to point out how the author of these lines 'has the honour of giving Wordsworth his hint for his "Intimations of Immortality in Early Childhood".' We all know this critic, but we also all tolerate him, honour him and pay him to torture us afresh instead of reminding him that literary history without coincidences would be unthinkable and that everyone with a spark of originality is always finding other people making epigrams or expressing ideas which he himself has up till that moment fondly imagined to be his alone. To take an example. Every Londoner now knows Maurice Hewlett's epigram that 'the great advantage of living in London is that you can get out of it'. Yet I will venture to say that a large number of us who live in London but who love the country as much as Maurice Hewlett have made that epigram before or after he made it public. Or again: not long ago Mrs. Annie Besant followed up an obviously original train of thought in a speech in the Queen's Hall, by the remark, 'is it not curious that a politician is the only person who does not have to be qualified for his job?' There was a good deal of laughter from the audience at this repetition of Bernard Shaw's remark – a sort of laughter which rather puzzled the speaker.

But I am convinced that Mr. Shaw himself does not care two straws about 'originality'. He often shows great appreciation of a writer who indulges in an open 'theft', while he himself often rejuvenates an epigram such as Johnson's 'Hell is paved with good intentions' or Wilde's 'there are only two tragedies in life; one is wanting something, the other getting it' – probably the two greatest and most profound epigrams in the language. And it is worth reminding the reader of how he once met the charge of taking his ideas from Ibsen and De Maupassant. There was a controversy upon this subject in *The Daily Chronicle* about twenty years ago. Into the midst of this controversy Shaw suddenly threw a letter. He never mentioned Ibsen or De Maupassant. Instead he proceeded to paint in detail the street in which he lived, the lives of the inhabitants who surrounded him, the sanitary accommodation for washerwomen and so on. He then spoke of the Vestry upon which he sat, of the sort of men who made up the committee and of how their ideals prevented them from descending so low as to think about washerwomen. After a survey of the situation he concluded – 'If a dramatist living in a world like this has got to go to books for his ideas and his inspiration he must be both blind and deaf. Most dramatists are.'

It is Shaw's knowledge of affairs that has made him appear such a singular or De Maupassant-cribbing dramatist. Shaw the vestryman is exalted above Shaw the playwright. But there are two incidents in Shaw's life which I have always been utterly unable to solve. Two dark problems. First, how *could Blanco Posnet* ever have been censored? Second, by what extraordinary means did Shaw manage to get himself elected as a Vestryman for the Borough of St. Pancras?[1]

---

[1] 'By a job. Never by fair democratic election. When I fought the opposition instead of having it squared for me, I was defeated.' G. B. S.

CHAPTER ELEVEN

Common Sense about Shaw's 'Immortality'

★

BERNARD SHAW does not fear death. Rather he rejoices in death as he rejoices in birth and has often declared that he expects to have a great feeling of healthy gladness when his time comes to die and make way for someone else. 'I am looking for a race of men,' he once said, 'who are not afraid to die.'

Now that is a very unpopular view for a dramatist to take up – for though we still like fighting and wars, we also like, in civil life, to pay a proper respect and becoming fear to death. But Shaw, fiercely reacting against Ibsen's suicides and shootings, refused for some time to conduct death on to the stage at all. This infuriated Mr. William Archer, Rationalist. He assailed Shaw for this weakness as he called it, in the *Daily Chronicle*. He insisted that if drama was the illumination of life, then no dramatist should neglect death which threw such light upon life. He appealed to the poetry in the pathos of the thousands whom 'a Greater Dramatist than Ibsen or Shaw continually condemned to suffering and extinction'. He implored Shaw to write 'a serious play' – that is to say a play with death in it. He cried 'While death is still the touchstone of character, the supreme test of fortitude, the refuge of despair, the consecrator of greatness, the desecrator of loveliness, the crass intruder and deliverer yearned for in vain, the matchless stimulant, the infallible anodyne, the signature to the stave of life, the mystery and the solution, the problem and the key, so long will dramatic poetry have recourse without shame to what is in fact the most penetrating searchlight in the armoury of her craft.' Shaw obligingly answered this challenging dithyramb by killing Dubedat in *The Doctor's Dilemma*. But his attitude towards death has remained unchanged. He will not take it sorrowfully; and he will not tolerate the idea that anyone could go on living for ever after death in another world — though in *Back to Methuselah* his Ancients have reached the stage when they can accept the burden of eternal life. He could not bear himself for longer than a long lifetime. He believes simply that the Life within him at death returns to the general source of life 'to renew the battalions of the future'.

And we find that Literary Immortality interests him no more than personal immortality. His values are quite different in this respect from most writers — Samuel Butler for instance. In his *Note Books* Butler tells us again and again (perhaps a little too often to be convincing) that he does not want much fuss made about him while he is alive, that a short span of fame beyond the grave is worth any amount of neglect and suffering before it, that a great writer's real life only begins in the next generation, nay, that he cannot be considered properly alive until he is thoroughly dead! I am convinced that Shaw is not in the smallest bit concerned about what posterity will say of him. He would much prefer fame in his own generation than in the years to come. That is simply a logical outcome of the fact that his attention is fixed more upon sociology than upon Art. He wishes to do service to his generation. He wishes to remove evil. Therefore he does not hesitate to write a play like *Widower's Houses* and then to harangue the audience in these terms – 'I heartily hope that the time will come when this play will be both utterly impossible and utterly unintelligible.' For it is part of the nobility of this man that he cares much more for the commonwealth than for himself and feels that if his work can do good in his generation it matters not whether it endures in the next. He laughingly refers to the time shortly to come when no one will read him because everyone will have caught up with his ideas. He is a standing proof that the last test of greatness is *not* what posterity is going to say about a man's work. Why should it be? It is a hasty assumption.

But will Shaw's work last only a short time? I do not think so. Shaw himself I am certain does not really think so either. There are two reasons why his work will endure as long as it is possible for Literature to endure. The first is of course because he has written beautifully. Beauty lasts. Thought is always being superseded but Beauty is everlasting and her lovers are not false.

Milton's thoughts are now out of date; but because he dressed them in such priestly robes we read them still. Shaw has likewise seen to the garments of his thoughts and so he cannot die.

But there is another reason why he shall walk with posterity. The historical interest of his work will serve to keep it alive even if its beauty fails to do so. We ought, by this time of day, to be getting tired of people who question the lasting power of Shaw's work on the ground that it is topical. It all has a date to it, they say: it is all about the passing moment, and the passing moment unfortunately passes: and so on. Let us call common-sense to our assistance and realise that it is because Shaw's work is topical that it will last, it is because it has a date to it that it will last, it is because much of it is journalism that it will last. When an author is dead for some time what is it that interests us most about his work? What is it that interests us most about *The Tale of a Tub, A Modest Proposal* or almost any other of Swift's works? What is it that interests us most about the work of Sheridan, of Ruskin, of Voltaire, of Rousseau and such like? Not their thought which is probably as dead as they are: not necessarily their wit which may be less easy for us to appreciate than for their contemporaries: but the historical significance of their work, the picture that they have painted of their time. All of us are naturally interested in history however much we may have been taught to believe otherwise by schoolmasters: and the true historians of the world are the artists and not the unreadable pedants whom we are forced to read before we have the understanding to refuse to do so. Sometimes in the case of pictures the historical interest is the only real interest. A Margaritone or a Cimabue does not appeal to us from the point of view of beauty, but our interest is very much aroused when we come to recognise with Ruskin that their works are 'the burning messages of prophecy uttered by the stammering lips of infants'.

It is in this way that I have always thought Shaw's work gains so much from the point of view of readableness in future times. For my part I never read the Preface to *Heartbreak House* or *Peace Conference Hints* without saying to myself 'what priceless reading this will be for posterity!' When people say in complaint of *John Bull's Other Island* that 'it has a date to it' I thank God for it, because the more a work of art has a date to it the more it can stand the test of time. Mr. Chesterton's remark that only those who try to be in front of their time will ever find themselves behind it, may or may not be true; but it is at least equally true that those who artistically paint their own time will always be accepted and read by other times for the obvious reason that they are trustworthy witnesses. Only work which has a date to it has no date to it.

I venture to ascertain that if and when the

millenium dawns, though in that Utopia there will be no striking workmen; no doctors — those understudies of Nature; and no politicians — those understudies of Common-sense; that nevertheless great interest will be taken in the reading of *Strife*, *Waste*, and *The Doctor's Dilemma*.

Of course a good deal of difference is made according to the amount and nature of a writer's ideas. Perhaps the less ideas he has the better. One of the reasons that ensures a long posterity for Shakespeare is that he has few ideas which can go out of date. His ideas are so vague that a clever journalist can make him mean anything required — as was proved by the fact that when the Centenary of his First Folio was celebrated recently all the different party papers quoted him as a champion of their creed. Militarists quote *Henry V* to prove that he was a believer in war: quakers quote *Troilus and Cressida* to prove that he was a believer in peace — and so on. Such elasticity (often called universality) greatly assists literary immortality if it does not add to personal greatness. Doubt is also useful ground upon which to build: it is upon the firm foundation of unyielding doubt that Ibsen's dramas stand.

But there is one other element in composition, which if a writer has it, seems always to assure his lasting fame — namely passionate conviction. Take the case of Milton again. We read him now for his beauty. But he wrote beautifully because of his conviction that every word of what he said was true. *Paradise Lost* would never have been written otherwise. He definitely believed all he wrote about the Expulsion of Satan and the Garden of Eden. The original strength of *Paradise Lost* is now its weakness. Economists talk of diminishing returns on an agricultural field, but the phrase applies still better to the dogmas of religion. Every year there is a diminishing return of interest in every dogma, for God fulfils Himself in many ways lest one good dogma should corrupt the world. Thus while no one now believes in the intrinsic value of *Paradise Lost*, while we turn away in horror from the celestial wars and in amusement from the good digestion of the Angel Gabriel, nay while we exalt Satan into the position of hero of the epic so that the first are last and the last first, we still delight in the poetry because of its beauty and beauty's companion conviction. Macaulay's *Essays* have the same quality which conviction gives to the work of genius. He has not much to tell us as regards exact truth, but he will last because he was convinced that what he wrote was just; perhaps he will last all the better because he was unjust, because he was biased, because he was violent, because he was partial, because he was rhetorical. And no man has ever written with greater conviction or greater sincerity than Bernard Shaw. He believes with Hector in *Heartbreak House* that his spark, small as it is, is divine, and that the red light over his enemy's door is hell fire. That alone, without the beauty and without the historical interest ought to carry his work down the ages.

CHAPTER TWELVE

Conclusion

★

It is impossible for me to close this book without making some general remarks about Mr. Shaw. In the foregoing pages I have praised him much. In the following pages I must praise him more. That is dangerous as I pointed out in the beginning of this book: it is also hard on me, because if you praise a person without also blaming him at intervals no one will listen to you. Luckily there have been parts of Mr. Shaw's work that have needed blaming rather badly. But not quite enough to give the necessary balance to this book: not quite enough to make the reader feel that I am a superior person. And so a few racy details of an immoral life on the Continent or some lurid pictures of household unhappiness would no doubt at this point greatly assist me in securing the reader's confidence in my knowledge and understanding of my subject. But I prefer to stay with the truth, and let it lend what value it can to this book.

Looking at Mr. Shaw as a person the most interesting thing about him is that he is a very ordinary man. Perhaps only those who have seen him will gather what I mean. He puts on no airs; he is never dramatic; he never strikes an attitude; he sits down in a chair with no gestures; he speaks in a matter-of-fact tone strangely different from his work; when talking to a group of people he lounges about and doubles up with laughter like a Dublin policeman; there is no finesse about his conversation (that is what he meant when he said that the conversation of Oscar Wilde was of a quality that he could not hope to equal), instead he just rattles on with his Irish accent. There is no pose, nothing studied about him — he is just an ordinary man. It is impossible to see him stand in the middle of a circle looking as someone has well described him 'like an agreeable Father Christmas' without saying to oneself 'Is *that* the man, is that the author of Lilith's lines?'

Now that is one side of Mr. Shaw, a side of which it would be absurd to deny the existence. It would be absurd to deny that he is bubbling over with laughter and gaiety, that he has a sense of humour far more acute than most of us. It is one side of Bernard Shaw which must always be remembered. It is as much the real Bernard Shaw as any other part of him. But there is another side of him of much greater importance, a part unknown to most and entirely neglected by the general public. Namely Shaw the Church-goer. The newspapers all now talk of Mr. Shaw being a very religious man but having no religion themselves they do not understand what they themselves mean by that term. They vaguely understand that Mr. Shaw derives no stimulation from the slaughter-house and snatches no pleasure from the bottle. They hear with amusement that he takes neither tea nor coffee, neither morphia nor opium, that he neither chews gum nor smokes tobacco, but they do not realise that he *does* take one stimulant: the stimulant as he himself puts it 'of going to Church' — when there is no service on. I have heard him say (in the laughingly matter-of-fact tone he always instinctively adopts in order to hide his feelings) that an empty Cathedral is the one place he can go into and pray and express his soul. And has he not written 'there I find rest without languor and recreation without excitement, both of a quality unknown to the traveller who turns from the village Church to the village inn and seeks to renew himself with shandygaff. Any place where men dwell, village or city, is a reflection of the consciousness of every single man. In my consciousness there is a market, a garden, a dwelling, a workshop, a lover's walk — above all a Cathedral. My appeal to the master builder is: Mirror this Cathedral for me in enduring stone; make it with hands; let it direct its clear and sure appeal to my senses, so that when my spirit is vaguely groping after an elusive mood my eye shall be caught by the skyward tower, showing me where within the Cathedral, I may find my way to the Cathedral within me.' And has he not protested how in the presence of a great Cathedral 'you forget yourself and are the equal of the beggar at the door standing on ground made holy by that labour in which we have discovered the reality of prayer'? Now I emphatically say that no one can hope to understand Bernard

Shaw or to have the faintest glimmering of what he is driving at unless they recognise this essential part of him — the ascetic mystic who walks with God. The more I read him the more I am convinced that the jovial gay part is real and does exist but exists in spite of and to the disadvantage of the more important part. He is so shy that the careless tone which he publicly adopts has become part of him and a real part, but nevertheless gaiety is utterly foreign to the Mystic who is at the bottom of all his work.

And more than this. I detect in the Mystic not only no gaiety but a spirit of intense sadness. Shaw is fond of Blake: remember Blake's words 'Excess of sorrow laughs. Excess of joy weeps.' In *John Bull's Other Island* there is great laughter and shouting over the death of the pig, in the house of Cornelius Doyle. 'I don't know how you can laugh,' says Nora. 'Why not!' cries Keegan. 'There is danger, destruction, torment! What more do we want to make us merry?' And the voice of Keegan is the voice of Shaw. It is this sadness which is the root of all his gaiety. He hates gaiety. 'My heart knows only its own bitterness,' he once said, 'and I do not desire to intermeddle with the joys of those amongst whom I am a stranger. I assert my intellectual superiority. That is all.' His gaiety is but what Mr. Godfrey Elton in a brilliant poem called 'the broken bits of laughter stuck about his heart': it serves to conceal from the public eye the man who with his Mrs. George would be 'A voice for them that are afraid to speak and a cry for the hearts that break in silence', and to protect the man who was not ashamed to admit that someone could be 'The cleanser and inspirer of his trampled spirit'. It is just the outward covering of 'his suffering sensitive soul' as George Russell once described him to me. His pseudonym is 'G. B. S.' And the comedy and tragedy of his life lie in the fact that not only were the jests of 'G. B. S.' taken seriously by the public but also that 'G. B. S.' eventually did become a real part of George Bernard Shaw and has never ceased to remain part of him to the utter confusion of the public and (I think) to the man himself. But Shaw is not a Shavian.

In an earlier chapter I pointed out how all his work is governed by the fact that he looks at the Universe from the point of view of a Natural Historian. It remains for me to show the more general effects it has upon him.

It accounts for many things. It accounts for his remarkable serenity. Think of Ruskin, driven mad with grief for the world in his old age, utterly broken in body and mind, gnashing his teeth in vain and finally sitting like a ghost waiting for the grave. Think of Carlyle: think of Frank Harris' description of him walking down Chelsea during the last days of his life, with the gait of a lost soul and an expression of such frightful sadness as to raise the inevitable question from the beholder 'What is the meaning of such impenetrable gloom? What is the matter with this man?' The answer is simple in the one case no less than in the other. Both of these men were 'sensitive suffering souls': and neither of them had any religion. They did not know what they believed: they were torn with doubts and questionings. They had nothing to support them — and so they suffered like the damned in hell. But Shaw, probably more sensitive even than they, has a religion to support him, a firm rock upon which all his work is founded — the religion of Evolution and the Life Force. He is therefore as strong in his old age as he was in his youth; strong with the strength of Jesus the greatest of the Jews. Yes, he is serene with the serenity of Christ before Pilate and with a greater serenity than Christ upon the Cross; for when his hour comes he will never have to cry, My God, my God, why hast Thou forsaken me?

His religion accounts for his lack of bitterness towards individual men or groups of men. He is for ever repeating that Hell is paved with good intentions not with bad ones. He wages unceasing war against cruelty and 'sport' — but he does not see the sportsman as a villain (as Ruskin did), rather he protests that they are no worse than himself and that none of the sportsmen he has met are ferocious while all the humanitarians of his acquaintance are ferocious. He wages unceasing war for Socialism, but he does not couple his request that we should be social, with violent attacks upon the Capitalist – rather he repudiates Marx and insists that capitalists are well intentioned gentlemen, 'every drop of their blood is so sweetened by charity that they pay starvation wages to their scavengers lest they should be compelled to discharge the worn-out men whom they have employed out of benevolence. All their finest instincts are jarred unendurably when their minds are dragged down from the contemplation of photographs of princesses to sanitary conveniences for women.' He has waged unceasing war against prison-reformers, but has never failed to salute the goodness of their intentions. A thousand other incidents big and small could be given. The result is that all his life he has unquestionably been feared by none and despised by many. The result is that though he is a very good businessman owing to cussedness and though his Fabian days proved that he could be a great leader amongst a picked body of men he could never be a public leader or draw many followers. For you cannot be a big leader without bitterness and rancour in your heart.

This religion of his accounts for three most remarkable traits – his utter lack of jealousy, power of paying compliments to his contemporaries, and his unique contribution to controversial manners. I state as a fact, as master of my subject, that you may search in vain throughout his work for a single line of jealousy (or for that matter, unkind word) towards any man or woman alive or dead. The constant gibe that he pays compliments only to himself is the reverse of the truth. He goes out of his way to pay compliments to as many of his contemporaries as he can—though I will admit that he is often unfair to dead men like Darwin: for Darwin after all was an enormously conscientious biologist, and displays complete familiarity with the comings in and the goings out not only of all animals but of all fishes, of all insects, and of all birds! But as a compliment-payer Shaw is unrivalled, lavishing praise upon everyone whether they be on his own side like Mr. Sidney Webb or Mr. Wells or on the other side like Dean Inge and Mr. Chesterton; praise ranging from such a phrase as 'a third (Barrie) too tender-hearted to break our spirits with the realities of a bitter experience, coaxed a wistful pathos and a dainty fun out of the fairy cloudland that lay between him and the empty heavens' to his criticism of Frau Fassbender's Elektra 'a deaf man could have watched her with as little sense of privation as a blind man could have listened to her'. His controversial method is always the same—completely purged of all bitterness and resentment. In his Roman play Pothinus asks Cæsar does he not resent the treachery of Cleopatra. 'Resent!' cries Cæsar. 'O thou foolish Egyptian, what have I to do with resentment? Do I resent the wind when it chills me or the night when it makes me stumble in the darkness? Shall I resent youth when it turns from age and ambition when it turns from servitude?' Let his enemies attack Shaw as virulently as they like but they will never get him to lose his temper: let the medical profession reply to his criticisms with the personal adjective tempered by the selected statistic and he will still reply with complete composure and good nature: let Mr. Henry Arthur Jones shout 'traitor', 'blackguard', 'viper' at him from the *Morning Post* and he will not hesitate to assure Mr. Jones that his friendship and regard for him are still unimpaired; let Frank Harris furiously accuse him of plagiarism and underhand dealing and he will eulogise Mr. Harris to the skies. I will venture to say that these particular traits in Shaw's character and method have a very salutary effect upon the world of letters: a far more salutary effect than the supposed bad effect of his conceited manner and self-advertisement — traits which I must again insist arise primarily and paradoxically out of his shyness and his desire to serve his own generation. No one but a born idiot would dream of imitating his manner — at least not for another two hundred years.

This religion of his accounts for the unity and steady power of his work. It has kept him out of blind alleys, has saved him from falling by the wayside and stumbling in the darkness, and has conducted him from triumph to triumph.

Finally this religion of his accounts for the fact that he cares nothing for happiness. He believes that life has no object — except itself. So he refuses to pursue happiness. He harps upon this throughout his entire work. From Keegan who writhes at 'the horror and tedium of pleasure' to Marchbanks who rushes out into the night with the secret in his heart of the folly of happiness; from Tanner who departs from Hell to escape from it to Mr. Jack in *Love among the Artists* who curses the few moments when he allowed himself to think of it; from Ellie who rejoices in the strength of those who have lost it to Shotover who groans at the misery of those who have received it, we find an unparalleled distaste for the pursuit of happiness. Again and again he denounces it from the lips of his best belovèd. Perhaps this trait has nothing to do with his religion at all. It may be just because he is an Irishman. This cry of pain at the thought of pleasure is very Irish. The Irish climate affects many people in the way it affected Larry Doyle. There is something in the mournful burden of an Irish bog and the baneful shadows which the mountains cast that often leaves a brand upon the burning hearts of her greatest men. However this may be, Mr. Shaw, instead of having written over his mantelpiece 'They say! What say they? Let them say!'[1] should carve the

---

[1] 'I utterly repudiate the motto. It was carved on the mantelpiece before I lived in the house. I should never have dreamt of putting it there. You know, don't you, that it comes from Holyrood? I attach so much importance

words of Napoleon 'Would I be what I am cared I only for happiness?'

I cannot hope to paint all the traits in Shaw's character. I can only mention those which I know to exist and which interest me most. I do not know much about him: but the more I learn the more I come to realise that the greatest thing that he has so far done is not his work but his life – that is probably why some of us have to admit, even to ourselves, that we hero-worship him, the other side idolatry. I do not know much about him for there is little material to go on outside his work – which by no means gives everything away. There is little material because no man has ever talked about himself so much and at the same time revealed so little. And I might add, shown himself so little. It puzzled people why he did not answer the calls on the first night of *Saint Joan*. It is because he dislikes the public gaze.[1] He very seldom answers a first-night call. But as for get-

to what people say that I have spent my life trying to make them say the right things.' G. B. S.

[1] 'Hardly consistent with my platform mountebankeries. I used to take calls when it was necessary to make speeches and fight the opposition; but since then I never take a call unless there are special and pressing reasons for doing so. Nobody but actors *in character* should ever appear on the stage: anyone else is a hideous artistic solecism and a betrayal of an illusion which should be sacred. Until "calls" are abolished they should be left entirely to the actors.' G. B. S.

ting him to say the truth about himself you might just as well be asking the same thing of Dean Swift who shared with Shaw the trait of always giving the wrong reason for most of the things he did. Gradually we will learn more from Mr. Henderson and (I hope) from the inevitable memoirs of Mrs. Shaw, but until the gates of Adelphi Terrace are opened and the iron bars on the stairs are cast down and Mr. Shaw gives us his promised (?) autobiography we will remain in the dark as to much of his character. Indeed as I write these lines I know that I really know nothing about him — and I doubt if his personal friends are much wiser. Bernard Shaw can never be seen by others alone with Bernard Shaw. I can only suggest that possibly the best clue to his inner nature can be found in Cæsar's speech before the Sphinx.

There are two incidents I can add that help to throw a little light upon him and therefore worth recording. The reader will be glad to hear that one is uncomplimentary. Nothing will ever induce him to say that he is wrong upon any point. When Carpentier was about to fight against Dempsey Shaw, remembering the genius that Carpentier displayed against Beckett, wrote to the *Daily News* saying how unfair it was for poor silly people to listen to the terrific backing that was going on at that time against Carpentier. The refrain was 'Don't lose your money, Carpentier is bound to win.' He lost. A year or so later a friend of mine approached Mr. Shaw on this matter in the language of reproach. But he insisted loudly 'I was perfectly right' — and then proceeded to show what things Carpentier had done wrong! The other incident is simply an answer to a question. Someone asked him if he would be our Dictator if Communism came to England. His answer was unreputation-like. 'I hope not,' he said, 'it would be with great reluctance and diffidence that I would take such a post.'

There are some people who are feeling anxious about Mr. Shaw at the present time. They feel that he is becoming disagreeably agreeable. They are afraid of him going soft. They say that they will assassinate him if he goes soft. A lot of people now hate to think that he is really a mild man just as in the early days others were deeply disappointed and offended to find that there was genuine knowledge behind his criticisms of music. I will admit that there is a great difference between the Shaw that was and is, between the young man of frenzied activity and the quiet serenity of these later years. But I must insist now at the end of this book as I did at the beginning that he is more revolutionary than he was when young and that his beard though venerable by no means signifies veneration. I admit that when I heard, all in the same week, that he had gone to Wembley, that he was bringing out a *de luxe* edition of *Saint Joan*, that he had been seen with a golf club, and that some newspapers were already beginning to call him 'The Master', I felt nervous – for it is only a step from this to opening a bazaar. But his recent reply to the O.P. Club on being invited to dinner has set me at ease and I can guarantee his would-be assassins that just as his view of the history of man will prevent him from going mad his sense of humour will prevent him from going soft.

In parting I would say this. Bernard Shaw can be appreciated in England better than anywhere else. His real home is England, not Ireland. It is not in Ireland that he is understood best – for he is Irish. It is not in Germany – for he is a classic there: and certain things convince me that the Germans do not really understand him in the least. It is hardly in Austria – for did not the Viennese believe that his mock-melodrama *Passion Poison and Putrefaction* was a serious work? It is not in America – for Americans travel much too fast to be able to think quickly, which is essential in order to appreciate much of Shaw. But in England, in spite of the thousands who are indignant with him because he mentions religion, and in spite of the gentlemen who assure us that some good melodramas are what he really ought to write, there is a much bigger public than in any other country ready to appreciate his subtleties and to accept his satire. For it is the great glory of the English people that in spite of all their faults they are perhaps the only people on earth who do not mind their short-comings being pointed out to them. That is why Mr. Shaw at bottom loves England: and that is why England will more and more come to understand Mr. Shaw.